Innovative Strategies
for Unlocking
Difficult Adolescents

Written by:
Robert P. Bowman, Ph.D.,
Tom Carr, M.S.,
Kathy Cooper M.S.W.,
Ron Miles, Ph.D.,
Tommie Toner, M.Ed.

© 1998 by
YouthLight, Inc.
Chapin, South Carolina 29036

Illustrations by Walt Lardner
Cover Design by Paul Neuburger
Project Layout by Melissa White
Project Supervisor Elizabeth Madden

ISBN 1–889636–07–X
Library of Congress Catalog No. (Pending)*

10 9 8 7 6 5 4 3
Printed in the United States of America

Table of Contents

The Nature of the "Difficult" Adolescents

What is the first thing that comes to mind when you think of the term, "difficult student?" For most educators, it is a picture of a student who has been particularly challenging to work with. Mostly, the difficult student displays behaviors that interfere with their learning, or the learning of others. These students are more demanding of the teacher's time and energy than other students.

Difficult students are those who continue to provoke or evoke unpleasant feelings in others such as:

Frustration

Annoyance

Anger

Sadness

Concern

Hurt

Fear

In other words, a "difficult" child is one who is perceived as difficult to reach for some reason.

Things to Remember About Difficult Students

1. **Difficult Students Evoke Unpleasant Feelings in Others**
   Difficult students are those who evoke the following kinds of feelings in those who are working to help them:

   > **Sadness** (disappointment to depression)
   > **Fear** (uncertainty to terror)
   > **Anger** (frustration to rage)

2. **A student who is difficult for one helper may not be difficult for another.**
   This occurs because the:
   - Student perceives one adult as more caring, accepting, understanding, trustworthy, and/or playful than the other.
   - Student unconsciously projects underlying anxiety to the adult and/or one or more other students in the classroom.
   - Adults have different tolerance levels for different kinds of student behavior.
   - Adult lacks critical information about the student or student's world.
   - Adult lacks the skills to reach the student.
   - Adult lacks the confidence to apply the strategies and skills needed for the student.
   - Adult has become personally invested and has lost professional objectivity or perspective in situation.

3. **Any student may be a "difficult student" at one time or another**.

4. **Some students become more difficult because they don't perceive themselves as valued by the helper.**

5. **It becomes much more challenging to think of an adolescent as "difficult" once you know his/her underlying story - and every adolescent has his/her story.**

6. **When developing an intervention plan for difficult students, remember:**

   - For persistently difficult students, educators should develop a team approach and not continue to "spin wheels" through the same efforts of one person.

   - Family members are important in the intervention process, but if they are not available, there are other people who might make a difference.

"High Risk"
vs.
"Difficult Children"

All "High Risk" students are not necessarily difficult. In fact, some high risk students are the opposite of "difficult." For example, the "teacher's pet" would not usually be considered by the teacher as a difficult student to work with. However, this student may be at risk socially and emotionally. Many of these students are "over pleasers" and are trying too hard to feel worthwhile through pleasing someone else.

On the other hand, not all difficult students are high risk. It is healthy and even expected that an adolescent will test limits occasionally. The adolescent becomes high risk when the intensity, frequency, and/or duration of these behaviors are significantly greater than usual for his/her age/grade level.

How then, should we define "difficult students?" Write some key terms below that you think should be included in a definition of this term.

Key Terms:

_____   _____

_____   _____

_____   _____

Difficult Students (a definition):

_____

_____

_____

_____

Underlying Causes of
Difficult Behavior
in Students

To understand a "difficult student" look at:

1. **Psychological Needs (based on Glasser's "control theory")**
   - Survival
   - Love/Belonging
   - Power
   - Freedom
   - Fun

2. **Environmental Contexts**
   - Family
   - Community
   - Culture
   - School and Classroom
   - Peers
   - Media

3. **Personal Characteristics/Traits (Myrick & Bowman)**
   - Physical
   - Social
   - Affective
   - Beliefs and Attitudes
   - Skills and Abilities

4. **Your Own Responses**
   - Communication Style (verbal and nonverbal)
   - Sensitivity
   - Objectivity
   - Reinforcement Patterns

Managing the "Difficult Classroom"

Sometimes a teacher is confronted not with just a few difficult students, but with an entire class that is exceptionally difficult to manage. It is interesting that when the most difficult student is removed from the classroom for a significant length of time, another student sometimes takes over the role left vacant. This is because some classes develop into strong systems that function more as a group than as individual members.

A system is more than the sum of its parts (1+1=3). To understand and transform a difficult classroom requires looking at the students as a system that contains the following three elements:

1. Persecutors
2. Victims
3. Rescuers

Like a healthy family, the well functioning classroom system contains open communication between all members, clear roles and expectations, mutual respect, and reasonable limits.

The Difficult Classroom

Characteristics:

A difficult classroom may be:
- Overwhelming
- Crisis centered and primarily reactive
- Overly noisy
- Hostile
- Violent
- Disrespectful
- Ambivalent
- Chaotic
- Unfriendly
- Nonaccepting
- Unresponsive

Underlying Causes:

1. School System
    - Lack of heterogeneous grouping.
    - Disproportionate number of dysfunctioning students.
    - Lack of support personnel for the class.
    - Lack of emphasis on cooperative learning.
    - Lack of staff teamwork.
    - Physical environment of the classroom.
    - Overcrowded class.
    - Toxic grouping - class group does not gel for unforeseen reasons.
    - Teacher lacks:
        A. Information
        B. Skills
        C. Confidence
        D. Objectivity

2. Family and/or Community
    - Sociological and cultural issues
    - Family issues
    - Multilingual grouping
    - Unrest
    - Violence
    - Life style (e.g., substance abuse)
    - Impoverishness (inadequate medical, safety, nutrition, or emotional support)

3. Extraneous Circumstances
    - Time of year - stress and excitement of holidays and end of school year.
    - Weather conditions.
    - Political & economic state of the country or region.

Strategies:

1. Involve parents and guardians.
    • Make lots of home visits and phone calls.
    • Send home lots of notes and letters.
    • Hold several parent-teacher meetings and be sure to separate the deeds from the doers and emphasize to parents positive qualities in their student.
    • Invite them to become involved in their school.
        - Active recruitment by PTO or PTA members
        - Mentors
        - Tutors
        - Storytellers
        - School helpers
        - Attendees in workshops and seminars held at school and/or in the community.

2. Start each year with a series of ice-breakers and team-builders which encourage students to build a cooperative momentum.

3. Set aside times for classroom meetings to discuss issues related to the class.

4. Establish the cooperation of the classroom in dealing with disruptive as well as positive behaviors.

5. Keep classroom rules to a minimum and word them in positive encouraging terms. Involve students in formulating the rules and consequences to build a sense of ownership.

6. Be consistent in enforcing rules and consequences, but not rigid. You can make occasional exceptions and still be fair because each student is different.

7. Provide the students with acceptable outlets for frustration or tension.

8. Watch what and how you command and confront the class. Many crises that occur in a classroom are triggered when a student feels backed into a corner and feels there can be no saving of grace.

9. When confronting, choose your words carefully. Use specific behavioral commands instead of judgmental statements. Provide consequences with a firm, but calm voice.

10. Agree with the students on a signal which will serve as a reminder when disruptive behavior begins.

11. When all else fails, try using appropriate humor.

12. Recognize times when the student or students are able to get along well in the classroom. Avoid saying that a student or classroom always behaves poorly. This may set up a failure identity or a self-fulfilling prophecy.

13. Avoid responding with anger or sarcasm. This tends to reinforce the idea that inappropriate behavior actually does get results.

14. Try to incorporate the negative experience into a positive learning experience for the classroom.

15. Assure to the student or class understand that it is their behavior, not them personally, that you are displeased with.

16. Help the student or class understand that they are responsible for their own actions.

17. Set up group incentives toward which the class can cooperatively work.

18. Provide choices for the student or class. Offer consequences as well as incentives which are motivating for that particular student or classroom.

19. The seating arrangement determines the patterns of communication within the classroom. Look at several alternative seating arrangements and change them as needed.

20. Use "time out" to isolate students, but allow them to return when they are ready to exhibit the desired behavior. Allow students to take "time out" on their own when they need it.

21. Use role-play, stories, puppets, or media to explore classroom cooperation.

22. Every staff member should have at least one person they can talk with at their school, openly and confidentially.

23. Find an ally. Each staff member should develop a collaborative relationship with another staff member.

24. Use the "Survival Skills for the Classroom Teacher."

Survival Skills For the Classroom Teacher

When all else has failed:

• Involve the class in a movement activity that regains teacher control.

• Use silence to help you regain composure and draw attention.

• Use a soft-spoken "broken record" approach.

• Use a time out for the entire classroom.

• Catch the students off-guard by doing something strangely unexpected.

• Call in your staff ally and swap classrooms for a while.

• Send a student, or small group of children, to your staff ally's room, not as a punitive act, but as a change of scene.

• Make sure you take care of yourself.

- Have at least one major outside interest that is not directly related to your work as an educator.

- Have one or more "significant others" to relate with outside of your work.

- Exercise regularly, and watch your diet.

- Keep learning new things and changing your routine. Don't allow yearly routine to build up boredom or complacency.

- Keep playfulness in your teaching style.

- Now and then, close your book and lesson plans, and teach spontaneously from your heart.

- Take a mental health day before you really need it.

"Control Tower"

PROCEDURE:

1. Ask for two student volunteers. One will be the "pilot" of a landing plane. The other will be the person in the control tower.

2. Blind fold the pilot as you explain that the instruments on the plane have failed and the control tower will have to "talk" the plane down.

3. As the pilot is being taken to the starting point, the leader sets up an obstacle between pilot and tower, using books, desks, chairs, book bags, and other items.

4. The control tower person stands at the opposite end of the "runway" and must tell the pilot how to land, or arrive at the control tower, safely.

ALTERNATIVES:

Other students may be lined up on both sides of the "runway" flicking their fingers like blinking lights.

FOLLOW UP:

Explore how the pilot and control tower person felt before, during, and after the activity. Also, what did the observers notice?

Lead a discussion about what each of the two students needed to complete the task safely.

Discuss the importance of open communication and trust in the school and classroom, as well as in a career and marriage.

"Electric Fence*"

PURPOSE:

To facilitate group cooperation in the classroom.

To teach problem-solving and decision-making skills.

To enhance an understanding of the importance of open communication and teamwork among students.

PROCEDURES:

1. Tie a rope from one chair to another so that the rope is a little lower than waist high.

2. Tell the group that their job is to get the entire group across the rope without anyone touching the rope. Should one member touch the rope, the team must start over.

3. Make participation optional and allow some students to take other roles such as group cheerleaders or referees.

VARIATION:

The activity could be done with an entire class at one time. Or, time could be saved by dividing the class into two or more smaller groups.

FOLLOW UP:

When successful, ask group members how they finally accomplished their goal.

Lead a discussion on how cooperation, communication, decision making, and problem-solving helped.

* Adapted from Weinstein & Goodman, Playfair

The Five "A's" of Helping
Students Connect

1. **Acceptance**
   - Accept the doer not the deed.

   - Accept the student's personal style.

2. **Attention**
   - Give attention at appropriate times.

   - Greet students

   - Listen to students

   - Check for feelings

   - Acknowledge what the student has said.

   - Teach students to ask for attention.

3. **Appreciation**
   - Remember, "The deepest principle of human nature is the craving to be appreciated." . . . (William James).

   - Tell students what you appreciate.

   - Describe the behavior specifically and accurately.

   - Occasionally write down words of appreciation.

4. **Affirmation**
   - Affirm with specific and enthusiastic comments.

5. **Affection**
   - Remember that one of our basic needs is to be loved and that affection breeds affection.

   - Use unconditional words and touches to communicate the value of each student.

© 1998, YouthLight, Inc.

From: Alpert, L. <u>Cooperative Discipline</u>

Facilitative Listening Skills*

1. Be aware of visual cues

- Your own body language

- The talker's body language

2. Listen carefully to the words

- So that if the talker would stop talking at any moment, you could always summarize what he/she had just said.

3. Listen to the feelings behind the words

- Note whether you hear primarily pleasant or unpleasant feelings or both

4. Say something that shows you are listening

- Use the high facilitative responses

(Adapted from Myrick, R. D. & Bowman, R. P., (1980). <u>Children Helping Children</u>. Minneapolis, Educational Media Corp.)

13

Three Helpful Responding Skills*

Open Questions (In particular, "What" and "How")

Clarifying/Summarizing

Feeling-Focused Responding

Encouraging Student Involvement

Encourage contributions of student to class.

Allow students to be helpers.

Give students choices in environment.

Ask for students' input for rules.

Allow students the opportunity to say positive things to each other.

Using Negotiation in Student-Teacher Conflicts

1. **Stop**

2. **Identify the problem**

3. **Generate ideas**

4. **Evaluate ideas**

5. **Develop a plan**

Special Concerns:

1. Hunt for win-win situations that will work for teachers and students.

2. Let students know their feelings are important.

3. Allow students to come up with ideas.

4. Write down all ideas.

5. Involve everyone affected by decision.

6. Help students understand the concept of choices as it applies to self-control.

7. Describe the behavior instead of evaluating it.

8. Be firm but friendly.

9. Control negative emotions.

10. Avoid escalating the situation.

11. Allow students to save face.

Interventions When the Student's Need Is Power *

1. When teachers acknowledge that they can't dominate, they can gain cooperation from students rather than confrontation.

2. Acknowledge the student's power. When we give up our power and control, the student has nothing to resist. People who feel dominated often react by resisting the person in charge.

3. Realize that teachers cannot "make" students do things. Realize that we can threaten, take away rights and privileges, and send notes home, but until the student chooses to do the work, it will not get done.

4. Remove the audience so that the student will not be reinforced by the crowd. Conflicts may intensify when others are watching to see who will win. More seems to be at stake.

5. Name the student's behavior and inform the student that you would be willing to talk or to discuss the matter in a calm voice. If this is not possible at the time of the conflict, make an appointment to do this later.

6. Use a "fogging" technique. Act as if the negative statements are of little or no value to you. Basically you are saying that you will not allow the student to manipulate you. Active listening will only prolong the confrontation.

7. Agree with the student as much as possible. This way the student has less to disagree with. (e.g. If a student says you're a horrible teacher, respond, "You may be right, now do problem #4.")

8. Use time-out in the school. The teacher may want to give choices, i.e. time-out in present room or in another teacher's room. (e.g. "Would you like to go alone or with another adult?")

9. Time-outs should be increased if behavior continues.

10. Use "when-then" statements. When you do this behavior, then _____ will happen.

11. Establish clear consequences. Appropriate consequences are:
    *   Related to the misbehavior. (e.g. "If you tip the chair, you will stand for the rest of the period.)
    *   Reasonable. (e.g. If the child scribbled on the door, reasonable consequences would be to scrub the door. But, to scrub every door in the building would be unreasonable.)

- Respectful and conscious of student's self-esteem.

12. Know the difference between consequences and punishment. Consequences reflect the above. Punishments are not related, reasonable, or respectful. Punishment provokes hostility and antagonism.

13. Jane Nelson describes the following results when using punishments instead of consequences.
   - Resentment: "This is unfair - I don't trust adults."
   - Revenge: "They're winning, I'll get even."
   - Retreat: "I'm getting away."
   - Rebellion: " I won't get caught next time."
   - Reduced self-esteem: "I'm a bad person."

* From: Alpert, L. <u>Cooperative Discipline</u>

Behavioral Strategies

Many at-risk students have behavioral problems, often severe enough to cause suspension, expulsion, and eventual dropping out. The following strategies, ranging from least to most severe, may provide help to classroom teachers and support staff:

- Ask small favors of offenders.
- Model the behaviors you expect.
- Give encouragement.
- Use modeling of others.
- Give support from routine.
- Use interest boosting.
- Restructure the classroom program as necessary.
- Use hurdle lessons.
- Provide for rule/consequence knowledge.
- Use group reinforcers and positive feedback.
- Use planned ignoring/differential reinforcement.
- Use proximity control.
- Use signal interference.
- Use direct appeal to values.
- Remove seductive objects form the desk
- Use the antiseptic bounce.
- Make direct requests for behavior change.
- Inquire about behavior.
- Use reflective statements.
- Alter the environment. (Move the student.)
- Have class meetings.
- Conference with the student.
- Use individual reinforcer.
- Use home reinforcer.
- Use peer buddies.
- Use contracts.
- Conference with parents.
- Counsel with student.
- Use saturation.
- Stay after school.
- Stay in for recess.
- Student can choose own consequences.
- Use Time-Out or remove from classroom.
- Use corporal punishment.
- Suspend student.
- Expel student.
- Referral to outside agency/medical.

Crisis Management
How To Help Those You Care About

1. Understand that emotional consequences follow a traumatic experience.

2. Don't expect that the person you care about will "get better" in a certain amount of time or in a certain way. Often recovery is a long and difficult process. If the person requires more time than you expected, you may feel frustrated or even angry.

3. Tell the survivor how you feel: that you are sorry they have been hurt.

4. Encourage the survivor to talk to you about how they feel. When they do, listen without interrupting or making judgements about what you hear. All the survivors feelings are okay even if you might not feel the same way.

5. Remind the survivor that their confusing emotions are normal.

6. Do not attempt to impose your explanation on why this has happened to the survivor. It probably won't be the explanation the survivor believes and imposing yours might hurt your relationship with them.

7. Do not tell the survivor, "I know how you feel" or "Everything will be all right." Often, these statements are really efforts to relieve your own anxiety about how you feel about what has happened to the survivor. Survivors say that when they hear these statements, they think that people do not care about or understand them.

8. Go to any court hearings, community meetings, or other appointments that relate to the trauma. This is an important way to provide support to the survivor.

9. Be willing to say nothing. Just being there is often all that you can do to help.

10. Don't be afraid to encourage a survivor to ask for help in the form of a post-trauma counseling. You might even go to the first appointment to show your support and concern.

The Process of Crisis Intervention

1. **Make contact at a feeling level.**

   - Identify student's feeling via active listening.
   - Accept student's right to feel in this manner.
   - Use statements rather than questions.

2. **Explore the problem now.**

   - Identify precipitating events.
   - Focus on immediate events.
   - Come to a joint understanding and description of the problem as it is now.

3. **Summarize the problem with the student so that you both agree on a definition of the problem's main elements.**

4. **Focus on the problem.**

   - Agree with the student on those areas where joint energies should be spent at this time.
   - Areas selected should be of most concern.
   - Areas selected should be susceptible to some immediate action with likelihood of results.

5. **Explore resources.**

   - Motivate and direct the student to tell you about what actions might be taken.
   - What would the student like to do, what is she afraid to do, who can be used as support, etc.
   - After student has explored resources, you can make suggestions.

6. **Contract**

   - Agree on plan of action with student.
   - Specify next step, what she will do, what you will do.
   - Specify goals,
   - Have clear methods for follow-up, emergencies, if necessary.

Immediate Post-Trauma
Debriefing

Post-trauma debriefings are most effective when they occur two to five days after the incident.

Debriefings should be mandatory for all persons involved in the critical incident and follow this format:

1. **Setting the stage**

2. **To begin the debriefings, any necessary introductions are made. The ground rules, including confidentiality, are discussed and the agenda presented.**

3. **Looking at the Consequences of Survival**
   Each debriefing participant describes their post-trauma situation - what their life is like at this time.

4. **Understanding the Consequences of Survival**
   Information concerning Critical Incident Stress is presented, including the normal results of the exposure to critical incidents and expectations for recovery.

5. **Contracting for Recovery**
   Each participant develops a plan for recovery that will assist in the management of Critical Incident Stress and reduce the possibility of long-term post-trauma stress.

6. **Closing and Evaluating**
   The debriefings include a follow-up session three to four weeks after the initial session.

Parent Coupon Booklet

One of the most frustrating aspects of working with difficult students is the lack of parental support. Quite often difficult students come from single-parent homes or low-income homes. These parents have a hard time getting to school during the day to see a teacher or participate in school activities because they are unable to get away from their jobs for a period of time. These parents often have low paying jobs and they cannot afford to lose two or three hours of work to come to school . . . this loss of hours may mean less money for food, gas, etc. The Parent Coupon Booklet is a practical idea that allows parents to leave work for a short period of time without losing pay.

The Parent Coupon Booklet Program

1. At the start of the school year, the PTO or PTA provides every parent at the school with a Parent Coupon Booklet. The booklet contains ten coupons. Each coupon is worth one hour off from work without loss of pay.

2. The school notifies local businesses, factories, industries and other employers in the area about this program. A letter encourages the employers to "support education" and allow employees to redeem the coupons so their workers can attend school during the day without loss of pay.

3. At the end of the school year, each employer who accepted the coupons are invited to attend a luncheon at the school to show the school's appreciation for their support. Business owners or managers are invited and they receive an attractive certificate from the school.

4. Also, throughout the school year, the local newspaper listed and thanked businesses for their support. Businesses like to see their names listed in the newspaper as supporters of education.

5. Some schools also add other coupons to the booklet. These "extra" coupons are for discounts and "freebies" from local businesses.

6. Another idea for this program is to place "redeemed" coupons in a box and have monthly drawings for prizes for parents who attended school thanks to the program.

7. Schools may wish to plan other activities around this program. The program has great potential to increase involvement and it gives businesses an avenue to show their support.

Attention Seekers

"Gossipers" & "Class Clowns"

"Attention Seekers" are students who are attempting to meet their need for attention. Many attention seekers are attempting to meet their needs for love and belonging, and, to a somewhat lesser extent, for power and/or fun.

Helpful Hints for Dealing with "Attention Seekers"

1. Do a flip-flop. That is, turn an attention-getting device into a learning experience.

2. Ignore whatever the child is doing.

3. Praise the child for something that has nothing whatever to do with his bid for attention.

4. Talk to the child privately about his/her ways of asking for attention. It may not have occurred to the student that that was what he/she was doing. Between the two of you, devise a check plan that will help him/her realize the extent of the attention-getting behavior.

Gossipers

Characteristics:

1. They may tell "stories" about others to peers or adults (less frequently).

2. Their stories may involve legitimate concerns, or be manipulative.

Underlying Causes:

1. They may feel the need to "elevate" their value as seen by others.

2. They may exhibit these behaviors as a means of getting attention from others.

3. They may not have the ability to solve, or cope with problems in other ways.

4. Their parents may have solved many of their adolescent's battles and thereby deprived the student of opportunities to learn problem solving concepts, skills, and confidence.

5. They may want to have fun and/or feel powerful by initiating conflict between others.

6. They may be striking out or seeking revenge at someone due to feelings such as hurt, anger, and jealousy.

Strategies:

1. Teach students acceptable reasons for gossiping, i.e., safety concerns or someone being hurt.

2. Avoid talking negatively about students yourself, in front of students or other educators.

3. Use cooperative learning.

4. Emphasize strength-building and affirmation activities in the classroom.

5. Don't overreact. Sometimes a lesser response will reduce the reinforcement of this behavior.

6. Teach students social skills for dealing with teasing, name-calling, aggressive attempts, etc.

7. Encourage independent behavior by rewarding pro-social skills.

8. Reward affirmations made by students in the class.

9. Use strategic humor to stop the gossip or tattling.

10. Teach "Refusal Skills" to help students refuse to be a link in the gossip chain.

11. Use "Share" (see next page).

Helpful Hints for Dealing with "Gossipers"

1. Ask the gossip if he/she is willing to put into writing the juicy morsel he/she just peddled to you.

2. Expect students to be positive, instead of negative, in their comments about others. Hopefully, the attitude generated in the regular classes will spill over into the students' purely social contacts.

3. Help students, through class discussions, learn how to cope with gossip when they are the ones gossiped about. They will be able to add to these suggestions: ignore the gossip; refrain from counter-charging; talk to someone you can trust; don't talk to everyone.

4. Resist the temptation to get "in on" the gossip that you sense is going around. Promptly discount 90% of what you overhear and put the other 10% into mental cold storage, just in case it proves significant later on. Knowing what you do, you may, in an ensuing discussion, diplomatically avert embarrassing situations.

"SHARE"
With Attention-Seeking Adolescents

Remember, adolescents will continue to behave in one particular way until some new behavior is learned. Most students are usually doing the best they can to meet their needs at the time. If "helpers" can provide understanding and support, difficult students can learn new behaviors and how to meet their needs in more effective ways. So, "SHARE" with your students—they can't change alone.

S Show the adolescent how to give and get attention in appropriate ways.

H Humor is something learned. Model and teach appropriate humor.

A Analyze the cause for the behavior. If it is attention, provide the adolescent with appropriate ways to get attention.

R Reinforce appropriate attention-getting behavior. Emphasize the adolescent's strengths and ignore silliness.

E Explore other strategies with the adolescent to meet the goal being achieved through class clowning or teasing. Enlist the group's help through planned ignoring.

"Behind the Scenes"

PROCEDURES:

1. Provide each student with an index card with a "label" of a particular kind of student on the front, and a description of that student on the back. Examples of possible cards include:

Gossip Label	Behind the Scenes
"Pregnant"	"It's not really true. I just went out with this guy and rejected him. Then, he started telling others I was pregnant."
"Alcoholic"	"I used to have a major drinking problem. But, I've quit and I'm going to AA meetings."
"Nerd"	"I wish others knew how painful it can be to be rejected by so many people, especially when I was abused so much as a child by my parent."
"Jock"	"Believe it or not, I have very low self-esteem. I work so hard at sports because it's the only way I know to feel good about my self at all."
"Bragger"	"I brag about things that I have and things that I've done because its the only way I think others will like me."
"Stuck-Up"	"I'm quiet and careful around others because I'm being cautious. I don't think I could ever handle being hurt by someone as badly as I was by someone at the last school I attended."

© 1998, YouthLight, Inc.

2. Next, the leader asks each student to place the card on his/her forehead so that the label shows to others. Note that the leader will need to hand the card to the student so that the label cannot be seen by the student. Each student should place the card immediately on his/her forehead, without looking at the side with the label.

3. Then, without revealing what is on other student's cards, everyone should walk around the room and interact with several others. Each student should be treated by others according to the negative ways students sometimes treat someone with their label.

4. Allow this interaction to continue for 5 - 10 minutes. Then ask students to return to their chairs, remove the labels from their heads, and read them.

FOLLOW UP:

1. Ask students to share how it felt to be treated as they were.

2. Encourage students to share in small groups their labels and to read the underlying stories on the backs of their cards. Then, they should discuss in their groups the importance of realizing what might be "behind the scenes" when they hear gossip about someone.

3. Ask students to explore how gossiping is like this game. For example:
   • Gossiping puts labels on people which may not be accurate.
   • Gossiping assumes information, sometimes exaggerates, and leaves out critical details of the story.

4. Discuss why and how gossip starts.

5. Explore what students can do to confront, or avoid gossip. For example, one strategy would be to confront someone when they are gossiping.

"Refuse the Gossip Game"

PURPOSE:

To teach refusal skills specifically for dealing with gossip.

PROCEDURE:

1. Have students sit in a circle.

2. Teach students the skills of "refusing the gossip."

    A. Use an "I" statement to share your feelings.
       (e.g., "I don't like to say bad things about others.")

    B. Suggest an alternative activity.
       (e.g., "Would you like to go play this game with me?")

3. Have one student be "it" and approach a student in the group and tell some gossip about someone else in the group that they make up.

4. If the person "refuses" the gossip, that person is applauded by the group.

VARIATION:

The whole group is divided into two teams; each team attempts to accumulate points. Points are earned when team members take turns acting out the gossip and successfully refuse it.

FOLLOW UP:

What different feelings do people have in gossip situations?

What is the peer pressure to participate in gossip?

What are other ways students could help stop gossip?

What are some difficulties students may find when trying to stop gossip?

Class Clowns

Class Clowns are students attempting to meet their need for attention by acting silly or foolish. Students may meet their needs for love and belonging, fun, and power by using this behavior. Remember, what did Charlie Chaplin, W.C. Fields, Cid Ceaser, Ernie Covacs, Freddi Prince, Jacki Gleason, and John Belushi have in common? These famous comedians and many more used their comedy, in part, to help them cope with deep troubles in their lives.

Characteristics:

1. They attempt to use humor to distract others in the classroom.

2. They may play "practical" jokes on others.

3. They may make distorted faces or make frequent unexpected comments.

4. They may display attention-seeking gestures or sounds such as giggling or simulating body sounds.

Underlying Causes:

1. They may believe they have no better way to solicit attention.

2. They may have feelings of low self-worth or confidence and may be seeking recognition.

3 They may have never learned appropriate humor.

4. They may be attempting to divert attention away from family problems such as alcohol abuse or family violence.

5. They may be attempting to cope with a class that is frustrating or boring to them.

Strategies:

1. Teach students appropriate humor by pointing out how things are funny to you.

2. Let the class clown know that you appreciate his/her humor, but make sure the student knows his/her "serious" side is also appreciated and important.

3. Give the student a chance to "shine" as a comic at a specified time.

4. Use "Attention Redirection." For example, develop a plan with the student that will help the student meet his/her comic needs, yet control them.

5. Help the student understand his/her need for attention and help find other ways, in addition to humor, to receive this attention.

6. Provide the student tasks that require intensive concentration.

7. Redirect the student's creative talents through activities like dramatics, games, and puppets.

8. Even if all the other students continue to laugh at the "class clown," don't overly react yourself.

9. Place the student in situations in which he/she can gain appropriate attention from peers.

10. Allow students to be in leadership positions.

11. Use seldom-tapped resources such as peer helpers and/or mentors to help the class clown to receive attention in the form of personal listening, affirming, and/or participative learning activities.

Helpful hints for Dealing with "Class Clowns"

1. Build into your schedule release times when it is OK to be the class clown without censure.

2. Give the clown responsibility that demands concentration. Find an isolated place for him to work. The task should make him feel important as well as convince him that you take him seriously.

3. Interpret the clown's goals for him. ("You crave attention and you feel clowning is the best way to get it.")

4. Praise the student about something that carries the inference that he's sensitive, not just a clown.

5. Preempt and redirect the student's disposition to clown.

"Calming a Comedian"

PURPOSE:

To redirect the class clown's behavior by appropriate opportunities for class clowns to use their talents for facilitating laugher in others.

PROCEDURE:

1. Hold a meeting with one or more class clowns together.

2. Acknowledge the talents and skills that these students have.

3. Lead a discussion with the students on the value of humor and when it may be a very positive or appropriate thing to do, and when it may bring troubles to them or others.

4. Invite these students to be leaders in the school by helping to organize one or more humor-based clubs, activities, or projects. For example, they might explore the following list and brainstorm other ideas to bring appropriate humor to the school.

   • Organize a "Comedy Club"

   • Plan one or more "Talent Nights"

   • Publish a booklet of "riddles, jokes, & funny stories."

   • Contribute humorous items to the school paper.

   • Schedule "Comedy Nights"

FOLLOW UP:

Have these students lead a classroom lesson on humor to younger students. For example, they might develop and deliver a lesson for middle and/or elementary school students.

© 1998, YouthLight, Inc.

"The Clowning Around Rap"

PROCEDURES:

1. Divide class into groups of three to five students.

2. Have students write a rap song together that talks about the negative effects of clowning and some positive alternatives to clowning.

3. Have students present these in front of the class and to other classes.

FOLLOW UP:

Ask students to describe a time they used clowning as a way to get attention.

Ask students to explore alternatives to being a class clown.

Manipulators

"Truth Benders" & "Game Players"

Manipulators deliberately misgive information or misguide someone to achieve some predictable payoff. Players become increasingly adept with practice and confident with success.

Manipulators often need power and want control. They have a goal in mind of how they want other people to behave or believe. Skilled players develop back-up plans.

Truth Benders

Characteristics:

1. They may make untrue statements which are either:
   - a simple reversal of the truth.
   - an exaggeration (magnification of the truth).
   - a fabrication (creation of an untrue story).
   - a confabulation (development of a story that is partly true and partly false).
   - a wrong accusation (blaming on someone else)

2. They have an intent to deceive to gain personal advantage or to avoid unpleasantness.

Underlying Causes:

1. Lying is an index to a student's feelings of being unloved or from feelings of inadequacy and pressure.

2. They may attempt to enhance themselves in front of others by claiming to do things which actually may not have occurred.

3. They may hope to gain the attention and approval of others.

4. They may strive to maintain friendships with other students.

5. They may be trying to get revenge on other students.

6. They may be attempting to fulfill expectations of significant adults who have labeled them as a "liar."

7. They may be striving to imitate the examples of other significant adults who may lie to avoid confrontations with others or to gain some positions as a result of such.

8. They may be attempting to escape dealing with painful memories or occurrences from the past.

9. They may be following modeled family values.

Strategies:

1. Confront the behavior based on the evidence at hand, making a statement to the student about the behavior. Do not demand that students testify against themselves by insisting on a confession. When questioned too harshly, students may feel that it is necessary to keep lying to avoid punishment.

2. Role model honestly by admitting openly to the students when you make mistakes. Be sure students trust in your honesty with them.

3. Teach honesty as an important virtue or value of daily living. Provide stories, dramatics, or puppets that illustrate the power of truthfulness.

4. Resist the temptation to moralize or preach because the student will "tune you out."

5. Convey the idea that you are more willing to remember the times a student told the truth than the time she/she lied.

6. Maintain a safe and encouraging classroom climate in which students are allowed to express ideas and make mistakes without fear.

7. Apply consequences cautiously for lying. It may be appropriate to include two consequences, one for the misdeed, and one for the lie, but be careful not to be too intense.

8. In the case of extreme exaggerations, do not react too much, but remember what was said. Listen especially to the feelings behind the exaggeration. These stories are the student's attempts to communicate some underlying needs to you.

9. Provide positive reinforcement for truthful acts.

10. Help students who bend the truth by using problem-solving techniques. If a student desires attention, brainstorm appropriate ways to gain attention. If a student desires to protect his/her friends, don't ask that student to be the sole discloser of facts. If a student fears failure, give the student adequate room to succeed.

Helpful Hints for Dealing with "Truth Benders"

1. Assure the child that he can depend upon you to tell him the truth.

2. Convey the idea that you are more willing to remember the times he told the truth than the times he lied. ("Phil, I'm sure it was difficult for you to admit you forgot to tell your dad to call me last night, but I'm so proud of you for admitting it." The assumption here is that the teacher and the student recognize the problem and are both working on it.)

3. Deal directly with the habitual liar instead of trying to trap him. ("Jim, you have Carrie's purse. Please return it to her.")

4. Evaluate your expectations of the student and try to discern the areas in which he feels compelled to lie. Does he, for example, lie about schoolwork? His dad's job? His mother's job? His wardrobe? His physical prowess?

5. Ignore those fantasy-oriented tales that probably have no serious consequences. ("My grandpa gives me $5.00 every time I go to see him." Even though you know his grandpa is on welfare, pass this up. Ignore it, but remember it for what it is.)

6. Read or tell stories that illustrate the power of truthfulness over falsehoods. Resist the temptation to moralize, because as soon as you do, you'll be tuned out.

7. Use normal consequences to help the student learn the benefits of telling the truth. ("You said you had finished and it's clear you didn't tell the truth; so you will have to forego the pleasure of _____.")

"Games & Lies"

PURPOSE:

To help students learn to detect "game playing," and lying.

PROCEDURE:

1. Divide the group/class into teams.

2. Alternating teams, one team member makes a statement which can be either true or false.

3. If the opposing team correctly guesses whether the statement was true or false, that team wins a point. For example, John, on Team A, states that he had dinner in New York City with a beautiful girl once. Team B must come to a consensus whether they want to say that John is telling a lie, or the truth. If they are correct, they win a point. If they are wrong, John's team wins a point.

4. Continue the game until one team reaches 10 points, or until time runs out.

FOLLOW UP:

Discuss how easy or difficult it was to identify true and false statements.

Have students share what strategies were easier to detect and which were more difficult.

Discuss the connection between "game playing" and "bending the truth."

"Media Lies"

PURPOSE:

To discuss "lies" that we see in the media and how they influence our lives.

To begin looking carefully at the messages sent to us from the media and the values they portray.

PROCEDURE:

1. Cut out pictures of advertisements and write on tagboard. Laminate.
   Examples:
   - A. People drinking in a van with a lot of friends, having a lot of fun.
   - B. Your brain is like an egg. This is what happens when you're on drugs - the egg fries.
   - C. The tidy bowl man.
   - D. The Nestea® plunge
   - E. Starburst®
   - F. Nike Air® commercial.

2. After each picture, the student is asked what the commercial implies. e.g., "If you drink beer, you'll have lots of friends and have lots of fun."

3. Is that the truth or an illusion?   If it is an illusion, as is the example above, what is the real underlying truth? (e.g., "If you drink too much, alcohol will damage your body, impair your ability to drive, impair your judgment, etc.

FOLLOW UP:

Talk about what kind of lies most people try to believe.
1. I must wear Calvin Klein jeans.
2. I must have Nike Air.
3. I need Bugle Boys
4. I must drink to have friends and to have fun.

What would happen if each of us told 10 lies each day?

Are all lies wrong or bad? Give an example to defend your point of view.

Game Players

Game Players are students who are attempting to meet their need for power and perhaps even love, belonging, and fun. They are adept at finding ways to control people and at learning which buttons to push to get what they want.

Characteristics:

These are students who:
- seek to dominate others.
- seek to play games by manipulating others.
- blame others for their problems.
- feel frustrated, angry and unloved when others will not behave as they want them to.
- complain and whine to get what they want. (very dependent students)

Underlying Causes:

They may play games to:
- protect themselves.
- get what they want.
- get out of doing things.
- cover up a perceived weakness.
- avoid being responsible.
- keep from looking bad or foolish.
- get other people to solve their problems.
- avoid an unpleasant situation.
- look good in front of others.
- get attention.
- get sympathy.
- avoid being asked.
- place blame on others so it won't be placed on you.
- be "better" than others.
- be pitied and "victims."
- prove how tough and/or wonderful they are.
- look important.
- get their way.
- get help.
- have others worry about them.

Strategies:

1. Present the concept of "con games" to students and differentiate these games from those that are more positive, like sports and board games. For example, "con-games" are plans that we might make to "trick" people into doing or not doing something. They are not honest.

2. Define and give examples of games.
    - acting tired to get out of doing the dishes.
    - acting busy so as not to have to talk to someone.
    - acting afraid to keep from trying something new.
    - acting like a bully to prevent others from knowing how afraid we really are.

3. Become "game-wise" and help students "restructure" their games.

4. Allow students to share games they have played with others.

5. Help students to learn to recognize their own games.

6. Help students to realize how they use games in various situations in front of various people.

7. Help students to realize how games help them get what they want or need from other situations. For example, games may help them manipulate others so that they can receive more love or attention or receive power and/or revenge.

8. Confront the student's game, state the behavior, and ask students if they would be willing to do the activity without the specific game.

9. Determine which games might be appropriate and which games might not.

10. Ask students to think of what things they want, for example, attention from teachers and having friends. Ask them to cut out of a magazine what they can do to get what they want. Students could also draw what they will have to do to get what they want in appropriate ways.

11. Ask students to make collages of their wants and/or needs. Discuss with students needs such as for love, acceptance, safety, and fun. Ask them to make a list of their needs, and then to choose three. Then ask them to draw and/or write ways in which they can meet their needs and wants.

12. Video tape or audio tape several games and let the students tell you what they're about.

13. Make puppets or masks to demonstrate games to others.

14. Watch a TV clip and point out "games."

"Becoming Game-Wise"

If the Game is:	The Underlying Need May Be:	A Suggested Intervention
Temper Tantrums	Power over adults; getting what the student wants.	Ignoring the behavior; time-out; not rewarding the behavior.
"Cool"	Power, attention, looking good in front of others.	Acknowledge the student for appropriate actions.
Helpless	To avoid being asked to do things; dependency probably inadvertently reinforced by adults in the student's life.	Encourage the student to complete the task. Do not buy into the "helpless" act. Reward the student for completing tasks. (May use a behavior contract.)
Bullying	To look important; To look "better" than others. The need for power. The need to mask insecurity. Anger about some issues. Poor social skills learned from a violent home.	Conflict resolution. Examine underlying causes (determine if a family intervention is necessary.) Teach social skills; reward peaceful resolutions to problems. (May want to use a behavior contract.)
"Don't Care"	Insecurity - fear of failure. To achieve recognition of self-worth.	Set up success identity - utilize motivational strategies. Re-ward any successful behaviors. Allow the student to be a helper to teach peers. Also, encourage positive self-evaluation.
Clowning	Attention from others, love and belonging, need for fun, masking a family problem like alcoholism.	Allow the student to gain attention in appropriate ways. Have a star search, comedy hour, etc. in the classroom. Reward appropriate behavior.
Stubborn	Power, freedom, testing the adult's ability for giving consequences.	Give student choices; do not allow the student to maintain control over the adult. Provide a choice with one being a natural consequence for continued behavior.

47

If the Game is:	The Underlying Need May Be:	A Suggested Intervention
I Can't	Avoidance of responsibility, dependency, fear of failure (probably reinforced by adults).	Do not allow the student to get by without doing the task. Do not buy into the attitude. Do not help the student every step of the way. Reward the student for trying. May want to use an "I Can."
Fearful	May indicate some traumatic situations. May use at home to control others. May use to avoid an unpleasant situation. May use to cover up weakness.	Acknowledge feeling; explore family situation if you are suspicious. Use rehearsal techniques and allow student to practice handling the fearful situation in a safe environment. Relaxation techniques.
Whining	Attention, power, feeling bad (needs not met).	Ignore, time-out, make sure needs are met.
Name-Calling	Need to elevate self; power over others; lack of appropriate social skills; attention.	Notice positive behavior; time-out; encourage empathy, teach social skills.
Cutesy	Attention from adults and/or other students.	Give student attention for appropriate behavior; Allow student to help others.
Blamer	Fearful of consequences; avoidance of responsibility; power.	Reward responsible behaviors; do not buy into the blame; allow the student to accept responsibility for providing a consequence for his or her behavior.

Restructuring Student "Games"

S State the current behavior or what the child is actually doing.

T Talk to the child about the preferred or desired behavior.

O Offer the child choices.

P Provide a consequence for continued misbehavior.

This model is a way of dealing with manipulative behavior. For example, if a child is whining, you might say the following:

1. State the behavior: "James, I've asked you to sit in your seat three times this morning. Here you are, out of your seat again."

2. Talk to the student about the preferred behavior: "I would like you to stay in your seat."

3. Offer choices: "You can continue getting out of your seat and be asked to leave the classroom. Or, you can sit down in your seat and if you would like, we can talk about it after class."

4. Provide a consequence: "If James chooses to continue getting out of his seat, the first consequence would immediately be provided."

Note that if "STOP" doesn't change the unwanted behavior in the other student, then there needs to be a back up plan, such as just walking away, or telling a teacher.

Hostile Students

"Sherman Tanks," "Snipers," & "Exploders"

Hostile students are those attempting to meet their need for power. Most hostile or aggressive acts are attempts to communicate feelings of hurt and inner pain. Some may express revenge or be a part of the grief and loss process. They are powerful because their behavior arouses confusion, mental or physical flight, and a sense of helpless frustration and leads to tears or rage. These acts rob the victim of the ability to deal with the situation calmly and competently.

Hostile students may take various forms. Aggression may be provoked or unprovoked or may take the form of a tantrum. Aggression may be physical or psychological or both.

Nine Tips on Being Angry
and Fighting Fair

When you feel angry you can:

1. Imagine a sign in front of our eyes. Put a stop to your growing anger. This may mean taking a deep breath, or walking away for a few minutes.

2. Identify your feelings to yourself. Ask yourself some important questions: What am I really angry about? Do I have a good reason to be angry with the other person, or have I been looking for an excuse to hurt him/her? Am I picking a fight because I'm in a bad mood? Or am I really mad at someone else but afraid to let that person know?

3. If you feel that you have to argue, make sure you choose your time and place carefully. Don't try to resolve arguments when you've got to go to class or you're about to eat lunch. If the other person persists, you might answer, "Look....(person's name), this is too important for both of us to spend only a few minutes on. I think we both need time to talk and listen. And even if you don't feel you need the time, I do. Let's meet after school when we have more time to talk."

4. When you do begin to talk with the other person with whom you have a problem, express your feelings without losing control of them. Use words like "I feel . . ." Do not raise your voice or move toward them in a threatening way. Stay calm.

5. Once you're talking, stick to one issue at a time. Don't tell them about their "momma . . ." It really does not help to use phrases like: "Yo mamma wears combat shoes, Yo big head, You weak, scoop-up head, or "peasey head." When you really want to straighten out the argument, **stick to the issue**. Don't blame or accuse the other person.

6. Express your point of view. Use the word "I." For example, instead of saying "YOU never listen to me," you might say, "I feel I'm not being listened to when I talk."

7. The secret of fair fighting is arguing not to win, but to seek resolution that works for both of you. You don't have to win - and see the other person lose - to get results. Both parties win of you can keep your self-esteem in a fight and learn something from it. For example, you don't have to call your friend names to let him know that it hurts to be stood up. Letting your friend know how you feel can help him change.

8. **Listen carefully to everything the other person has to say!** If your friend tells you she is late because she always comes by your house to get you, it may be time to meet halfway between her house and yours.

9. **Forgive**...once the argument is over. Forgiving is letting go of the anger that sparked the fight. Then a handshake, or hug, is good way to end an argument. **Get on with your life.**

52

How to Handle
Conflicts Constructively

There are three ways to deal with anger:

1. You can "stuff it." But if you stuff or hide anger, you may become withdrawn or depressed. And one day you might explode.

2. You can "escalate it." But if you blow up, blame others, and call them names, your anger has a good chance of working up into violence. That's the worst way to handle your feelings.

3. You can "direct it." When you say to someone, for example, "I feel angry when you're late," you're directing your anger squarely and taking responsibility not only for resolving the conflict, but for making yourself feel better.

**Even if you have problems with your anger, . . .
You can still learn to fight fair and get results**

Group assignment: Each member of the class writes one sentence describing one thing that happened recently which made the class member angry:

Sentence: _____

_____

Volunteers read their sentence aloud to other members of their class. It is not necessary to discuss the sentences at this point with the class.

Group Activity: Allow class members to offer helpful suggestions for the situations read aloud by the volunteers.

Unique Strategies for Dealing with the Angry/Aggressive Student

Most of the following strategies will be useful in dealing with students from upper elementary school to high school. For younger students, teachers should use time-out and redirection as much as possible. Teachers at all levels may have to refer the "angry" student for counseling, conflict resolution, social skills training, and/or extra help outside of school.

Use of "Matter of Fact" Approach

When dealing with the angry student, it is important to remain as calm as possible. The angry student is probably used to hearing parents and others yell and use loud voices. The student probably expects the teacher or adult to get loud with them. By using a calm, level-headed approach, it may actually help the angry student to begin to "cool down." Teachers who use the "passionate" approach of discipline with the angry student may actually be making things worse.

Escape Passes

The angry student needs to begin to control his/her anger and be more responsible for his/her actions. This strategy offers the student a way to avoid getting angry and to escape, temporarily, from the situation that is causing the anger. The student is given a certain number of cardboard/paper passes. When the student begins to get upset, he/she may give the teacher one of the passes. This allows the student to leave the room for a few minutes. The student may sit in the office, go to the library or use the bathroom. Once the student is "under control," he/she returns to class. The passes usually are for only three to five minutes.

Redirection List

The teacher keeps a list of errands at her desk. When she notices a student starting to get angry, she looks at her list of errands and has the student complete the task. Suggestions include: take articles to office, take note to another classroom, check the teacher's mail box, etc.

Manipulatives

Some teachers allow the angry/aggressive student to use manipulatives at their desk. As long as the student is not being too loud or distracting others, he may use manipulatives at certain times during class. The best kind of manipulatives are the ones that take a little power or pressure to put together or take apart. This keeps the student's hands busy and it burns off some of his/her "extra" energy.

Teach Self-Talk

Encourage the angry student to use self-talk. Have the student practice this method. Some teachers actually write affirmations or "self-talks" on a 3" X 5" card and tape it to the student's desk. Statements could include: "I can handle this, it's no big deal," "I'll survive," "Tomorrow will be a better day."

Getting in the Last Word

The angry student always wants to "get in the last word." Some teachers allow this (as long as the last words are not disrespectful) while other teachers are determined that they (the teacher) will "get in the last word." Try this approach; **invite** the angry student to "get in the last word." For example, during a confrontation, say to the student, "I know you wish to get in the last word, so go ahead and say what you wish." By doing this, the student feels he/she has gained some power but really you, the teacher, has the power because you allowed the student to finish. Quite often when you try this approach, you catch the students "off-guard" and they do not know what to say.

Taking a Stand

When dealing with the angry student, it is important not to stand too close to the student . . . this becomes a threat. Also, do not confront the student face-to-face. Stand to the side and talk to the student. This means little eye contact. A face-to-face, eye-to-eye confrontation with an angry student would not be advisable.

Take a Humor Break

One teacher keeps a mask and a funny-sounding horn at his/her desk. When he senses too much stress in the room or if he/she notices a certain student getting angry he quickly puts on the mask and blows the horn. Students usually start to laugh. The horn means that the teacher tells a funny story, reads a joke, or asks a silly trivia question. This tactic can do much to defuse a tense situation.

Empathic Assertion

This calls for the teacher to make a statement to the angry student in such a way to let the student know that the teacher is aware of the situation and is aware of just exactly what is making the student angry. For example, the teacher might say, "John, I know you are disappointed you didn't make the team after practicing as much as you did," or "Sally, I don't blame you for getting angry, Erin should not have said that." By letting the students know you understand where "they are coming from," you can actually lessen the chances of a major outburst.

Fogging

Fogging is a way of confusing provoking parties by appearing to agree with them. When a student says," You're the meanest teacher I've ever had," respond with, "Thank you for the compliment" or "You're probably right." If a student makes a "not-so-nice" comment about your clothes, say, "You really think I have no taste."

The Pressure Point

This is one method that I have found successful with several students who had difficulty controlling their anger. I trained the students to recognize certain things that caused them to get angry. As soon as they witnessed or heard something that caused them to get angry they were immediately told to press their thumb and middle finger together, firmly, for ten seconds. By delaying ten seconds, the students were able to "calm down," think, and not over-react.

A Call for Help

If you have an angry/aggressive student in your room, you may need to come up with a plan of action to get help when necessary. Seek the assistance of a student in your class. Let Tasha know that when you look at her or call her name and pull on your right ear, she is to go for help as soon as possible.

STP

The STP Theory works well with students in grades 2-5. The famous racecar driver Richard Petty uses STP oil to keep his car "Running Smooth." Students are trained to use their STP when they get upset and are not "running smooth." When a student gets angry, he pretends to take his STP.

      S - Stay Cool
      T - Think
      P - Practice (teacher gives students suggestions for solving problems)

The Two-Minute Warning

Allow the angry student a short period of time to calm down. Don't try to reason with him/her when he/she is very angry. If the student doesn't settle down in two minutes, he/she may be asked to leave the room.

Let's Make a Deal

Many angry students show improvement through the use of written contracts. The contracts need to be short term and positive. The student can earn special privileges for controlling his anger.

Everybody Needs an Ally

Let the student know that you wish to help her . . . you're not her enemy, you're her ally. Offer to listen/talk with her after class. Suggest professionals, churches, classified staff and others who are willing to help. Find out what interests the student has. It is amazing what a pack of basketball cards or a poster can do to build a promising relationship.

Tom Carr, 1994

Suggestions for Handling Hostility in Students

Look for the Antecedent

Hostile behavior is usually quite predictable in that there is usually an antecedent to indicate future acting out behavior. An antecedent may be a change in the student's behavior or it may be the beginning of a "bad mood" for the student. It may begin with the student yelling out or dropping a book. An appropriate response might be to tell the student that you realize they are upset and that you would like to talk with them after you have started the class in an activity. At this time, you can talk to the student outside the classroom and make a plan for the student to deal with the hostile feelings before they become more explosive.

Use Verbal Decoding

Instead of assuming every action is against you as the teacher or counselor, use reflective listening to get at the underlying message. For example, if a student drops their books, the teacher might respond, "It looks like you're upset today."

Be Direct and Succinct

Moralizing, lecturing, and long rationalizations will not "sink" in to a student who is extremely angry. Short, succinct sentences or commands work best.

Use the Student's Name

If a student is upset, they may not be acting and behaving as they normally would. To use a student's name over and over, has a way of calling the student back to who they are.

Back Away From the Student

Most teachers tend to approach students when they are angry. This may appear threatening. Take a few steps back and hold your hands to the side. This is a universal peace sign and is much less threatening.

Do Not Appear Frightened of Student's Anger

If teachers appear frightened, scared or anxious, students will know they are in control. Always send the message that the school and you are in control.

Do Not Tolerate Any Signs of Graffiti in the School

Paint, wash over, and get rid of anything obscene or suggestive of student or gang power in the school. This establishes the mood of who's in charge. Don't let it be the kids.

Have a School Plan

All teachers need to know what to do in case of a fight. Several teachers should always respond. One should remove the rest of the class. One should remove dangerous objects. One or two should try to calm down the fight by the least restrictive methods first. Some teachers should know therapeutic holds for restraining students if necessary.

Use the Student Councils

Most students do not like fighting either. Involve the school in coming up with a plan to deal with disruptive students.

Maintain Structured Rules

Aggression occurs less in structured environments. Permissive environments tend to encourage hostile behavior.

You're Right

To deserved criticism, responding with "you're right" serves to prevent the conflict from going any further. To undeserved criticism, saying "you're right" but adding the excuse. It is also important to follow these statements with appropriate plans to correct the action.

Have Dress Codes

If gangs or weapons are problems, establish dress codes to prevent gang paraphernalia from becoming too obvious in the school.

Invite the Students to Talk With You

Sometimes merely taking time to talk with the student will go a long way towards solving any problem.

Have a Fight Form

Develop a form that has particular sections for information on it that must be completed by students. The form must have several primary components including the following: statement of the problem, contributing factors to the problem, how students intend to alleviate the problem and signatures.

Watch the Atmosphere You Create in the Classroom

Competition increases conflict. Allowing cliques to develop increases conflict. Encouraging children to win at all costs encourages conflict. Allowing a non-supportive atmosphere encourages conflict. Frustrating a student by placing unreasonably high demands on students encourages conflict. Labeling some students as "bad" before they are given a chance can encourage conflict. Expecting students not to get along encourages conflict.

Have a Fight Plan

Break up the fight. Get help if the kids are too intense or bigger than you. Don't expect or demand that the kids talk right away. Give them a place to have a time out either inside or outside of your room. Work out a plan when children are calmed down.

Methods of Working It Out

- Mediating - Each child can tell their side and both can suggest solutions.
- Fight form - See description
- Teach the children to be assertive.
- Use I statements.
- Use a calm voice.
- Watch body language.
- Use behavior contracts.
- Use non-verbal cues.
- Use problem solving techniques.
- Use classroom meetings.
- Use group incentives.

Plans for Dealing with the
Extreme Hostile Student

1   Reward other children for ignoring the child who is having the tantrum. Reward the "hostile" child for each period of time he/she does not have a tantrum. This can be done with a behavior contract. Whenever the "hostile" child has reached a certain number of stars of points, have a class reward or party. If giving out treats, allow the hostile student to pass them out. (Social reinforcements and peer pressure help to reduce the tantrums.)

2. Give a time out for the child with the tantrum. For every 90 minutes of tantrum free behavior, give the class a treat allowing the "hostile" student to pass out the treat.

    Greenberg, D.J. and O'Donnell, W.J. "A note on the Effects of Group and Individual Contingencies upon Deviant Classroom Behavior." Journal of Child Psychology and Psychiatry, 1972, 13, 55-58.

3. Allow an opportunity for the child to release pent-up energy. Jogging for 10 minutes may reduce aggression by up to 50% with the maximum benefit being after the first hour.

    Allen, J.I. "Jogging Can Modify Disruptive Behaviors." Teaching Exceptional Children, 1980, 12, 66-70.

Sherman Tanks

"Sherman Tanks" are students who display their attack weapons and armor clearly for all to see. They are openly hostile and the quicker people realize this, the better for them, according to the student

Characteristics:

1. These students may be openly:
    - abusive
    - abrupt
    - intimidating
    - overwhelming
    - arbitrary
    - arrogant
    - assaultive
    - critical
    - argumentative
    - antagonistic

2. These students may refuse to display much impulse control, choosing to ignore the rights of others.

3. These students may gain power through their abilities to arouse confusion, fear, and hurt in others.

Underlying Causes:

1. These students may be holding a lot of inner pain and are unconsciously attempting to resolve and heal their wounds by striking out at others.

2. These students may respond aggressively due to poor impulse control when a need is not met.

3. These students may be experiencing violence or neglect in their families. Insensitive acts and violent outbursts may be the only coping skills modeled for these students in their homes.

4. The media, as well as some rock groups, "glamorize" violence as well as "normalize" violence as a means of dealing with problems. (See the following section, "Television Violence.")

5. Alcohol and drug usage lowers ego control and induces impulsivity.

6. Many boys tend to believe that violence is the earmark of their masculinity and somehow "proves" something. Current gang activity supports this theory.

7. Lacks discipline and hostile attitudes from parents, may lead to poorly controlled students.

8. Students may respond angrily to loss or grief.

9. Students may need to prove to themselves and others that their view is right.

10. The hostile student's view of his/her world is absolute - clear and concrete, straight forward and simple.

11. These students think more in terms of "shoulds" and "musts" instead of "cans" and "wills."

12. These students lack empathy and trust that causes overuse of aggression.

13. These students may demean others to create sense of self-importance and superiority. "If I can make you out to be weak, faltering, or equivocal, then I will seem, to myself and others, strong and sure."

Strategies:

1. Teach social skills or appropriate ways to deal with anger.

2. Limit exposure to TV and rock group violence.

3. Encourage parents to try to work out differences in amiable ways.

4. Encourage parents to provide consistent limits and consequences for negative behavior.

5. Students should be encouraged to explore and discuss negative feelings.

6. Reward desired behaviors.

7. Ignore as much as possible unless the behavior poses a physical threat to the safety of another.

8. Teach assertive responses.

9. Teach problem solving or conflict resolution skills.

10. Help students learn self-control by learning to relax, count to or use self-talk.

11. Provide consequences for negative behavior.
    • Time-out is good
    • Take away privileges
    • Make restitution to the injured party. If the student is young and a blow was rendered, one may ask the student to pat the injured area for a while.
    • Physical punishment would probably be counter productive.

12. Offer more positive male models who handle aggression in a positive manner.

13. Foster feelings of empathy.

14. Make sure you look for underlying causes.

15. Do not fill "Sherman Tanks'" expectations by exhibiting fear or rage or be put out of commission. Avoid open confrontation.

16. Stand up for yourself. Use the Broken Record and/or Fogging Technique(s).

17. Give them time to relax. Breathe deeply and "center" yourself. Look directly at the yeller.

18. Don't worry about being polite, just get into the conversation. Be factual and calm. "You interrupted me." Smile.

19. Get attention carefully. Use the person's name; do something unexpected - drop a book. Be cautious of body space; don't look like you are going to attack.

20. Get the student to sit down. "If you are going to argue, we might as well be comfortable." Maintain eye contact.

21. Speak from your own point of view. Use phrases: "In my opinion . . . ," "I disagree with you." Paraphrase and summarize.

22. Avoid a "head on" fight or power struggle. You may lose the battle. If you win a fight, you may win the battle but lose the war!

23. Be ready to be friendly. "Stand up" to the bully and he'll be your friend.

24. Have a "cool down" time.

25. Use "diffusing" by focusing for a while on just the facts through summarizations and open ended questions.

26. Use "yielding" in which you refuse to "push back" at the student when provoked. Instead, encourage the student to use words to "let it out" while you listen. This may need to be at a planned location and time.

27. Sit down.

28. Be a good listener to the student's feelings.

29. Do something surprising such as offer something to drink.

30. Remain calm and state that you cannot talk at the present time.

31. Leave the scene.

32. Consider settling differences through "arm-wrestling."

33. Use films, books, puppets and drama to promote objective thinking about fighting.

34. Prevent fights by establishing ground rules such as, "when two students are fighting, the students watching will remain silent."

35. Redirect the hostility by combining a reprimand with a dignified command.

36. Conduct a small group meeting of four to six students to confront and listen to the "Sherman Tank." Make sure to pinpoint and include a discussion of his/her feelings, too.

Television Violence

By the age of two or three, most children regularly watch 26-33 hours of television each week.

Of all households, 98% have at least one TV turned on an average of 6 hours per day.

In an average evening of television viewing, deadly weapons appear about nine times per hour.

Of all prime-time network dramas, 75% contain some act of physical, mental, or verbal violence.

40 percent of all prime-time TV shows are considered to be very high in violence.

The average child has watched the violent destruction of more than 13,000 persons on TV by the time he/she is fifteen.

At current rates, the average American will view 45,000 murders or attempted murders on television by the age of 21.

The typical American child sees on television 75,000 incidents of drinking by the age of 21.

Of parents, 78% have used the television as a "baby sitter" at one time or another.

By the time of high school graduation, most children will have spent 11,000 hours in school, but more than 22,000 hours in front of the TV.

Robie, Joan Hake. Turmoil in the Toy Box II.

"Non-Violent Alternatives to Fighting"

PURPOSE:

To teach nonviolent alternatives to dealing with hostile attacks from other students.

PROCEDURE:

1. Make a spinner by cutting a circle out of poster board with a brad attached to the center.

2. Copy or rewrite the following alternatives on the edges of the spinner.

Walk away

Use humor   Do something fun

Try talking   Exercise

Change your seat   Relax your body

Take some time

3. Ask each student to draw a picture or write about something that makes them very angry.

4. Allow the student to take turns drawing a card and spinning the spinner. Each student is then asked to describe how the alternative that he/she landed on could be used to solve that problem.

VARIATIONS:

Use the activity in a learning center, small group, or with the entire class.

Divide the class into small teams and have each team earn points for appropriate answers.

FOLLOW-UP:

Discuss what anger really is (it is an emotion that you can feel in your body).

Have students make paper "anger thermometers" that can show how angry they are at any given time.

Have students draw large bugs and write in each "things that bug me."

"Anger Pictures"

PURPOSE:

To raise student's awareness of alternatives and consequences of actions taken during moments of anger.

To help students learn different ways of coping and dealing with anger.

To teach decision-making and problem-solving skills.

PROCEDURE:

1. Ask each student to divide a piece of paper into four equal sections (either with drawn lines, or by cutting to form a booklet).

2. Ask the students to draw each of the following on one of the paper sections.

   A. Draw a time when you were very angry and did something that hurt someone.

   B. Draw the person after they were hurt.

   C. Draw something that you could have done better so that no one would have been hurt.

   D. Draw what would have probably happened after you did that.

FOLLOW UP:

Ask students to discuss their responses with other students and brainstorm other possibilities for part "C."

"Snipers"

"Snipers" are students who may hide their attack weapons and armor. They carefully look for, or set up attack opportunities. Then they patiently lie camouflaged, waiting for the attack. These students may also be very adept at setting "traps" for others to get caught in.

Like rocks hidden in snowballs, they come at you softly, but hit you hard. They may sound like innuendoes, subtle remarks, digs, non-playing teasing. The victim feels pinned down as if there are no response choices at all. He or she is hit by well-placed verbal missiles, high-powered enough to hurt.

Characteristics:

1. These students are passive aggressive and display hostility covertly.

2. These students may talk behind a student's back with a smile.

3. These students may display incongruencies between verbal and nonverbal messages such as:
   • smiling and rolling the eyes for other students to see when the teacher, or another student does something well.
   • showing a "thumb down" or other negative gesture when someone else in the classroom does something well.

4. These students may provide subtle verbal put-downs.

5. These students may give "hook" compliments.

6. These students may be more effective than "Sherman Tanks" in striking out or hurting others because they are more subtle.

7. These students have developed more skills than "Sherman Tanks" for striking out at others, so that they maintain more control of the situation.

Underlying Causes:

1. Like "Sherman Tanks" these students have firm, self-centered views of how others should behave so that the "sniper's" needs are met.

2. These students may have deep feelings of hurt, frustration, and/or anger.

3. These students may need to strike out at others, and have learned that subtle aggression keeps them safer than blatant hostility.

4. These students like to win, and will work very hard not to lose. They like to be in control of a situation.

5. Like "Sherman Tanks," these students may be holding a lot of inner pain and are unconsciously attempting to resolve and heal their wounds by striking out at others.

Strategies:

1. Teach students to use positive self-talk.

2. Encourage students to look at themselves in positive ways:
    -"I Can" Books   -"I'm Special"
    -"I'm Thumbody"   -"All About Me" collage

3. Teach affirming activities:
    -"Balloon Game"   -"Batman Cape"
    -"Mailbox Game"

4. Use strength bombardment activities.

5. Help the student focus on accomplishments rather than failures.

6. Involve students in collaborative assessment and evaluation procedures.

7. Teach students the "Superman Shield" as a coping skill.

8. Teach students how to use "comebacks" when they are "cut-down":
    *   Ask the "sniper" what he/she meant by his/her comment.
    *   Be tactful and up-front.
    *   Say what you think the "sniper's" words mean, and then ask if you are right or wrong.
    *   When the "sniper" makes negative comments in the group, seek group confirmation or denial of the criticism.
    *   Consider underlying causes of the "sniper's" comment.
    *   If there is group consensus that a problem exists, set up regular problem-solving strategies.

9. Teach students how to look, listen, and reach out for allies (peers and/or adults).

10. If you are a third party to the "sniping," stay out of the middle but insist that it stop in front of you.

11. Take some "think" time.

12. Plan a time to talk about it. Say, "I really need to talk with you. Is there a time to talk? I really need to get my thoughts together."

Helpful Hints for Dealing with "Snipers"

1. Call the name-caller and his target together for a report of the experience. ("I'd like to have you fill me in on this name-calling episode. Since my memory is sometimes rather faulty, I hope you don't mind if I use the tape recorder." The playback can be very sobering.)

2. Hold a class meeting for the express purpose of discussing name-calling.

3. Hold a joint conference (aggressors and victims) to thrash out differences by drawing up a minimal, mutually agreeable plan: "You've now all agreed to hold the name-calling down to a minimum. John will report to Mr. Jones after recess on the progress of the gang; Jim will report to Mr. Hurley on his feelings. You say you want to try this for a week and you're willing to sign this contract."

4. Ignore the matter, at least for the time being.

5. Meet privately with the aggressor and state directly that name-calling is an act of aggression that is saying "Help!" Then proceed to elicit the student's fears and the reason that he/she feels compelled to lash out against the victim. ("Jenny, you're a bright girl. I don't have to tell you that calling others names is your way of crying for help. What's bugging you so much that you have to do it?")

"I Think 'Knot'"

PROCEDURE:

1. Find an open space such as a gym, cafeteria, or outdoors.

2. At some strategic time before the activity, ask one student in each group to be a "resister." That is, he/she will resist group suggestions and attempt to talk the group into believing the activity will not work.

3. Students should form groups of five to ten students (5-7 is best the first time). Make sure one "resister" has been placed in each group. Then, have students in each group stand in a circle facing toward the center.

4. Ask all students to reach out both arms and grab the hands of two other people (not the same person or someone standing next to them).

5. Once everyone is connected, ask them to untie their knot without any student releasing his/her grip.

6. After each group has experienced the effects of the "resistor," ask all groups to stop. Reveal the "resistor" in each group and lead a discussion about how a resistant student can sabotage group efforts.

7. Next, have each group attempt the task again, this time without the resistance. In most cases, each group will untie into a large circle. There are a few exceptions, however. In rare occasions, the group could end with an impossible knot, or two or more intersecting circles. Many times, however, if the group is persistent, they find that what they believed was impossible really wasn't.

FOLLOW UP:

Were you able to untangle yourselves without pushing, shoving, shouting, or bossing?

At what times might a fellow student be a group resistor?

How might a group minimize the effects of a "resistor"?

When might a group resistor be very important to the group? What can the group do to ensure resistance is "heard."

"Balloon Bash"

PURPOSE:

To help students to learn to give affirming statements to each other.

To help build student group cooperation and cohesion.

PROCEDURE:

1. Ask each student to blow up a balloon and write his/her name on it, or draw his/her face.

2. Ask all students in the group to begin batting their balloons up into the air. and try to keep all of them from touching the floor or ground.

3. When you give the signal, each student is asked to catch a balloon that belongs to someone else.

4. Then, each student is to find the original owner of the balloon and affirm them by saying something positive about them. Then, repeat from step "2."

5. After two or three times, ask students to eliminate any mention of looks or clothing. From this time on, all affirmations must be about something the person has said, or done.

FOLLOW UP:

Ask students how it felt to receive affirming statements.

Discuss what made this activity difficult or uncomfortable for some and easy for others.

"Exploders"

Characteristics:

- hostility
- fighting
- personal injury to another(physically or psychologically)
- hitting
- biting
- kicking
- throwing objects
- pushing
- spitting
- name-calling
- teasing
- profanity
- pushing
- temper tantrums
- impulsive
- irritable

Underlying Causes:

1. Temper tantrums are designed to manipulate adults into submitting to a student's demands.

2. Students may learn aggressive behavior as a result of modeling by significant adults or older siblings.

3. Students may be angry as a result of severe emotional upheaval such as abuse, divorce, death, etc.

4. Students may be angry and act out resulting from a psychological need for power.

5. Students may be overtly rewarded for aggressive acts by parents or others who require students to "take up" for themselves.

6. Students may be frustrated by tasks they are required to perform.

7. Students have watched violence on TV programs and hence "model" after their "heroes."

8. Students may be exposed to violence in their culture and grow to imitate it.

9. Music often speaks of destruction and disrespect, and students may model it.

10. Students and/or others in their families may abuse alcohol or drugs which may lower inhibitions and increase outbursts.

Strategies:

1. Utilize students' potential for leadership, assertiveness, and independent thinking by teaching them to use personal power appropriately and make effective decisions.

2. Avoid and defuse direct confrontations.

3. Grant students legitimate power.

4. Parents should maintain fun and loving discipline setting consistent limits.

5. Exposure to violence should be limited by parents.

6. Marital strife should be minimized by parents taking appropriate steps to deal with conflict.

7. Students should be encouraged to pursue interests that make them "happy."

8. Teach appropriate social skills and alternatives for dealing with difficulties.

9. Reward desired behaviors through use of behavioral contracts and/or verbal praise.

10. Teach assertiveness in such a way that students can learn to take care of personal needs while coping with others.

11. Discuss actions and consequences on TV.

12. Provide consequences for continued acts of aggression.

13. Utilize "time out" procedures for student to teach appropriate self control.

14. Provide appropriate male role models who obtain "power" in nonviolent ways for boys.

15. Help students learn to understand the concept of empathy.

16. Teach students how to discuss their feelings when they are hurt or angry.

17. Teach negotiation skills.

18. Show serious intentions. "I can see this is very important to you, but I cannot accept that you (tell specifically what the student said or did)."

19. Suggest that parents:
    • Give each student special time. Use activities chosen by the student.
    • Ignore undesirable behavior unless the act is hurtful to self or others. Offer choices to the student for alternative acts.

20. Provide logical and natural consequences such as:
    • Loss or delay
      - of privileges
      - of participation in an activity
      - of using objects or equipment

- Loss of freedom of interaction
  - denied interaction with other students
  - required interactions with school personnel
  - required interactions with parents
  - required interactions with police
- Restitution
  - repair of objects
  - replacement of objects

21. Use the five steps for deflating your own anger.
   - Step One: Acknowledge your feelings.
   - Step Two: Never act impulsively.
   - Step Three: Gain control.
   - Step Four: Explore options.
   - Step Five: Respond in a reasonable manner.

22. Use activities to help students deflate their anger.
   - Therapeutic stories
   - Balloon story
   - Role play
   - Draw a picture of something that makes you mad.
      - Draw two options of something you could do.
      - Draw a picture of you doing the option.
   - Make an anger plan and stick to it.
      - Clay
      - Dramatic play
      - Teach stress management
      - Have each student make his/her own "Anger Booklet."
        Topics include:
        - Think of someone on TV who gets angry.
        - Draw a picture of what they do when they're angry.
        - Draw a picture of someone else you know who gets angry. Draw what they do.
        - Sometimes we might get in trouble for what we do when we get angry. Draw a picture of what gets us in trouble for our angry feelings.
   - Draw 3 things you can do that won't cause you trouble when you are angry.
   - Draw a picture of your friend trying to get you to fight.
   - Draw a picture of the way you feel when you're not in trouble.

23. Use the "Feedback Model" (Wittmer & Myrick, 1990)
    Step One: State the specific behavior (action) that bugs you.
    Step Two: Say how it makes you feel (angry).
    Step Three: Say what you wish (want) the person to do instead.
    Example: "When you take my pencil without asking (action or behavior) it makes me angry (feeling). Please do not take it until you check with me first (consequence or result)."

Helpful Hints for Dealing with "Exploders"

1. Appeal to the child's ego with a matter-of-fact statement. ("Barbara, nobody enjoys the Barbara that throws tantrums, but everybody enjoys the helpful Barbara.")

2. Apprise the child of what he can expect from tantrums. ("Billy, tantrums are bothersome to everyone. Don't expect to get favors with them.")

3. Discuss with the student harmless ways of having a tantrum. ("The next time you feel a tantrum coming on, you may use the punching bag in the gym.") Solicit other "harmless ways to "throw a tantrum" from the student and his/her peers.

4. Explain to the child, at a time when he is calm, what the consequences will be the next time he has a tantrum. ("Jerry, perhaps this situation will never happen again, but I want you to know what will happen if it does: I will leave you alone until you stop screaming.")

5. Use nonverbal modes of coping, such as signaling the other students to quietly follow you out of the classroom and closing the door behind you.

"How Do You Spell STRESS?"

PURPOSE:

To help students explore alternative ways to respond to certain situations.

To teach students to learn their own style of coping with situations and how they can learn new approaches.

To help students brainstorm together different approaches.

PROCEDURE:

Give the following scenarios to students and have them discuss in small groups how they would respond, and then explore alternative ways to respond.

Some students start talking about your "Moma" and you hardly know them. What do you do?

The teacher confronts you in front of the class about the "F" you received on a test. How do you respond?

Riding with some friends, you discover they are planning to "hit" a convenience store. You want to fit in, what do you do?

Every time you call your best friend and try to get together, your friend makes excuses for why he/she can't get together with you. You sense something is up. What do you say to him/her?

Some students are planning to play a joke on a student who is very shy and doesn't have many friends. What do you do?

Several people approach you with drugs at a party. What do you do?

FOLLOW UP:

Ask students to talk about what the outcome would be in each situation.

Have students discuss a time that they experienced a similar situation.
What happened? How could you have approached it differently.

"DEFLATE" Your Anger

Deflate deserved criticism by saying "you're right."

Explain that you are going to leave if they continue.

Face them with a smile - don't let them see you down.

Laugh or use a little humor.

Answer "put downs" with "come backs."

Talk to yourself - don't believe what they've said.

Ease your way out of the situation.

"One-Minute
Madness Management"

PURPOSE:

To give students quick coping strategies to "head off" temper explosions.

PROCEDURE:

Bubble Trouble

1. Give a student a piece of bubble gum.

2. Tell the student to pretend the gum is the source of his/her anger.

3. At the start signal, the student should begin to chew the gum slowly and then increase the pace faster and faster.

4. After one minute, the students should blow bubble after bubble in a way to let the anger go."

Shove It!

1. A student positions him/herself against the wall.

2. The student is to pretend that the wall is the source of his/her anger.

3. On a signal, the student pushes his/her hands, arms, shoulders, back against the wall for one minute.

The Running Rage

1. Each student pretends that the source of his/her anger is not far in front of him/her.

2. Then they are instructed to begin running in place after this "source."

3. Students start slowly, pick up their pace, and then run as fast as they can for one minute.

FOLLOW UP:

Discuss after each activity how it may be a better alternative to "exploding" their temper.

Ask students to discuss how and when they might do any of these activities.

Have students brainstorm other ways to "head off" a temper explosion.

"Win/Win" Guidelines
For Conflict Resolution*

Take time for cooling off if needed. Find alternative ways to express anger.

Each person states their feelings and the problem as they see it using
"I messages." No blaming, no name-calling, no interrupting.

Each person states the problem as the *other person* sees it.

Each person says how they themselves are responsible for the problem.

Brainstorm solutions together and choose a solution that
satisfies both - a"Win/Win" solution.

Affirm your partner.

* From Drew, N., <u>Peacemaking Skills in the Classroom</u>

Apathetic Students

"Unmotivated Students" & "Daydreamers"

These students, unfortunately, are sometimes labeled "lazy." But, there are always reasons behind apathy in students, and discovering these reasons can open new possibilities in helping them to spark an interest in learning. Apathetic students see little or no personal meaning in their school work and are viewed by their teachers as uninterested, discouraged, and/or distracted.

Estimates of underachievement have ranged from 15% - 45% of all students with 75% being boys (Bruns, 1992). These students can be from disadvantaged homes, but many have parents who are highly educated. Many have average, or above average achievement test scores.

Displaying apathy can be a controlling mechanism which allows the student to dominate the time of the teacher or parent. It encourages the adults to feel guilty that they aren't there enough for the student. It also perpetuates dependency in the student and a blockage of success experiences.

Helpful Hints for Dealing with "Apathetic Students"

1. Help the apathetic student regularize his or her jobs so that he/she takes care of things on a schedule instead of trying to do them all at once. (What is best done right after school? Before the evening meal? On Mondays? On Sunday afternoon?)

2. Refrain from bailing the student out of situations that arise due to apathy. If you do, you are enslaving yourself to a problem that holds little promise of going away by itself.

3. State clearly what is expected by you. "You may do_____ after you have finished_____."

Eight Ways to Increase Motivation in the Classroom

1. Make sure each student succeeds every day.

2. Emphasize what the children are learning rather than their performance.

3. Make lesson presentations interesting and relevant.

4. Link learning to student's interests. State objectives. Tell students how this applies to their lives.

5. Offer students choices and opportunities for autonomy and creativity.

6. Keep presentations alive by adding variety to routines.

7. Mix learning styles.

8. Find ways students can interact.

Practical Tips for Motivating Students

1. Utilize counselors, mentors, exceptional teachers to help find "weaknesses" of students. Make a plan with the student emphasizing practical, reachable goals in incremental steps.

2. Find out sources of frustrations. Find peer helpers and mentors to teach students how to achieve success in deficit areas.

3. Allow at-risk students to teach someone else something.

4. Find out what students want to work for and help them attain it.

5. Help students feel comfortable with other people in the classroom.

6. Use cooperative learning and paired learning strategies.

7. Utilize classroom competition with other classrooms through the use of academic games or attained goals.

8. Set reachable goals for the class and offer crazy, or zany rewards for achievement.

9. Have students come up with weekly goals. Make it worth their while to obtain the goal. (Reward, prize, etc.)

10. Have weekly classroom goals. Example: Everyone will bring in their homework this week. We will all make 100 on the spelling test.

11. Try to arrange multiple goals for children. For instance, keeping out of trouble will get a student recess every day, a star on the chart, a chance to go to the 9 weeks trip, a good feeling about oneself, help the class obtain a goal of free time or earn a class trip, etc.

12. Make it worth the class' time to work toward their goals.

13. Maintain a positive, highly responsive classroom environment.

14. Use emotion as a motivator when necessary.

15. Tell constant bragging stories about children.

16. Have weekly awards ceremonies featuring some accomplishment of the student for that week.

17. Have a hobby day and let students share something they do well.

18. Go after small change.

19. Treat each student with great respect.

20. Encourage students to care about each other.

21. Maximize the individual's contribution to the classroom.

22. Believe that all students can learn.

23. Do not have students always competing against each other.

24. Have a talent show.

25. Show how subjects relate to the real world.

26. Allow students to teach the class.

27. Keep a file of significant achievements that the student has gained. Allow the student to add throughout the year.

28. Give students opportunities to brag on each other every day.

29. Notice when students help each other and make a big deal out of it.

30. Make journals and allow students to write of accomplishments, times they helped others succeed, and notes of progress in academics.

31. Give students pats on the back. (Activity in Gossiping section.)

32. Have school wide incentive systems.

33. Have a student of the week and learn about individual students.

34. Have a parade of excellence.

35. Have a monthly birthday party.

36. Recognize class achievements over the intercom.

37. Make sure students feel "invited" to be at school.

38. Send home cards or positive notes occasionally.

38. Send home cards or positive notes occasionally.

39. Give students jobs to do around the school.

40. Use students names often.

41. Make sure students get to know each other.

42. Tell students you miss them when they're out

Motivation
Systems Theory

1. Remember that you are dealing with a whole person.

2. Goals, emotions, and belief systems must be influenced and examined.

3. Realize that a student must have goals if they are to succeed.

4. Realize that multiple goals will strengthen motivation to complete tasks.

5. All goals must be attainable and realistic. They must make sense to the student.

6. Feedback must be given for goals to continue to be maintained.

7. Look for underlying reasons that goals may not be maintained.

8. Look at the environment to see if it is truly responsive to the student.

9. Use emotions as a motivator if necessary.

10. Check out belief systems that may be inhibiting goal attainment.

11. Treat each student with respect.

Adapted from Ford, Martin E. Motivating Humans (1992), Sage Publications.

Mystery Motivators

The following are several ideas that can be used by teachers to help motivate students. These activities will help students become more excited and motivated. By adding a little "mystery" in the classroom, teachers should see improvement in behavior and academics. Most of these activities can be adapted for use in grades two through high school.

Brown Envelope

On Monday the teacher places a large brown mailing envelope on a wall. A question mark is placed on the outside. Only the teacher knows what reward or treat is mentioned on the inside. Based on the classroom's weekly objectives, those students who earned a reward or treat get to open the envelope to find out what they earned. The reward could be extra playtime, extra computer time, ice cream, homework passes, or a "Pop Corn Party." This activity tends to be successful because the students do not know what they will earn until Friday afternoon. Two or three times a year, the teacher may include a rather big or unusual treat . . . this adds to the excitement.

Caught Being Good with a "New Twist"

Teachers, principals, and other faculty and staff members carry "Caught Being Good" tickets. When they spot a student doing something good or if they feel a student deserves some special recognition, they give that student a ticket. The student must then take the "Caught Being Good" ticket to a special location to redeem (i.e., counselor's office, school secretary, P.E. teacher). The student redeems the ticket by playing a game of chance. he/she gets to throw three dice and add up the points to determine the prize. The prize list is posted and it includes small prizes and at least one big one. A student can win a big prize by throwing "three ones" or "three sixes." Below is a sample prize list for a middle school. A special note here is that recently I used this list at a middle school and during the year only two students won the big prize (cassette tape or CD) but every student who earns a card knows that they have a chance to win a big prize. About 75% of the students will roll a number between 7 and 13 (small prize or a "Sorry.")

Total of Three Dice	Prize/Award
3	Cassette tape or CD
4	Candy bar and a free toss
5	Candy bar
6	Pack of gum or trading cards
7	Pen or pencil
8	Pen or pencil
9	Pen or pencil
10	Sorry (piece of candy)
11	Sorry (piece of candy)
12	Sorry (piece of candy)
13	Key chain or ruler
14	Key chain or ruler
15	Pack of gum or trading cards
16	Candy bar and a free toss
17	Two candy bars
18	Free pizza or dinner coupon for two

Grab Bag

Place a box or barrel in your class. Have it filled with envelopes or small brown bags. Inside each bag is a small prize. Make sure the barrel includes one "big" prize . . . . this adds to the excitement. Students earning a treat gets to pull out a bag. Prizes may include such things as homework coupons, free ice cream, McDonald's coupons, candy, extra playtime, etc.

The Spinner

Make a large circle board with a spinner attached. Students earning a reward or treat get to "Spin the Spinner" to determine their prize. Make sure your circle board contains at least one big prize.

The Candy Bar Game

Put together a large booklet that contains the wrappers from about thirty of today's most popular candy bars (Crunch®, Mars®, Milky Way®, Twix®, Mr. Goodbar®, etc.). At the start of a class or at the start of a day, place a candy bar in a brown bag (only the teacher know which candy bar is in the bag). At the end of the class period or at the end of the day, each student who had good behavior gets to guess which candy bar he/she thinks is in the bag. Before the students guess, the teacher shows/reads the Candy Bar Book for the students. The students must guess only the types of candy bars listed in the book. In case of a tie, the teacher flips a coin . . . there can only be one winner. Students must know that they lose their guess if they misbehave. Every day the teacher places a different kind of candy bar in the bag. The winner keeps the candy bar.

How Many in the Jar?

At the start of the week, the teacher places a jar on his or her desk. The jar could be filled with beans or candy. The class decides on a weekly objective (behavior, completing homework). Each day, the students who achieve objective earn a ticket. At the end of the week, each student turns in his or her tickets. Each ticket is worth one guess on "how many items are in the jar." The winner gets the contents of some other prize. The winner is the one whose guess is closest.

Let's Make a Deal

This activity is based on the old TV game show. Every once in a while a teacher may decide to play this game to add even more excitement/challenge. After a student has earned a reward or special privilege, invite him or her to play, "Let's Make a Deal!" If the student agrees to play then he/she must return their prize and select what's behind, "Door No. 1, Door No. 2, or Door No. 3"; the teacher may use envelopes or cards instead of actual doors, or curtains. The student is taking a chance because one of the three choices is bound to be a silly or worthless prize, but one of the three choices is going to be worth more than his or her original prize.

Trivia

On Monday, give your class a challenging trivia question. The students have until Friday to give you the correct response. A correct response could earn five extra points on a test, free homework pass, etc. Students love trivia questions and will usually work hard to find the answer.

Jeopardy

Students enjoy playing Jeopardy. Teachers can select the categories which can include geography, sports, music, science, etc. Students may have to earn the privilege to play Jeopardy on Friday. To add some fun/mystery to the game, place a star behind one or two of the Jeopardy answers. If a student gives the correct response to that answer then they win a bonus prize.

Wheel of Fortune

On Monday, the teacher places a chart/poster on the wall with a number of missing letters, during the week the teacher will allow certain students to turn the letters or buy a vowel. On Friday the students who earn the privilege will try to guess the phrase. A correct response can earn a prize.

Transition Tickets

Quite often teachers have classes that have difficulties during times of transition (going to lunch, changing classes, etc.). The teacher has a large roll of tickets. Each time the class has to go somewhere, the teacher passes out tickets to those who cooperated. At the end of the week or month, the teacher allows students to redeem the tickets for "mystery" prizes or privileges.

The Principal's Round Table

Purpose:

The purpose of the Principal's Round table is to randomly select a small number of middle school or high school students to meet with the principal to discuss various school-related issues. The "round table" allows students to get together to meet, talk, and discuss school issues. By randomly selecting students, the principal will have a group composed of students who would generally not talk or meet each other in school. The freshman would be mixed with seniors, males with females, students from different parts of town and county, and students from different cultural or ethnic backgrounds. By mixing groups, students will have the opportunity to meet new people, discuss social problems encountered by their peers, talk about school safety, peer problems, as well as other issues. The goal is that they will gain a better understanding of others and realize that they often share the same concerns. It is hoped that new friendships will be made which will result in a decreased number of conflicts, fights, or disagreements among different cliques or groups.

Method:

1. Each week the principal will randomly select approximately eight students form the school's roster. Each student is notified by receiving an invitation in the form of an attractive card from the principal.

2. The Principal's Round table will meet at the same time each week and the principal and a counselor or a teacher will meet with the selected group for two class periods.

3. All participants will sit in a circle.

4. Some schools choose to name the gathering after the school's mascot. Therefore, instead of being called the Principal's Round table, it could be called the Tiger Round table or the Cougar Round table, etc.

5. Refreshments (usually soda, chips, and/or fruit) will be served.

6. At the end of each session, participating students will receive a button (I was a member of the Cougar Round table) and a cup, water bottle, or T-shirt that displays the school mascot.

7. The principal will serve as a facilitator and will bring a list of discussion topics to help get the group started. The questions could be about the likes/dislikes of high school, current events, school violence, peer issues, etc.

8. The principal will take notes on important topics.

9. All students who attended at least one roundtable meeting will be eligible for a drawing to be held at the end of the year to receive prizes supplied by local businesses.

Benefits:

1. Increase in school spirit.

2. Decrease in stress and conflict among different groups of students.

3. Opportunity for students from various backgrounds to meet in a pleasant environment and develop new friendships.

4. Opportunity for students from various backgrounds to see that they often share similar concerns.

5. Opportunity for students to see the principal in a different role and to see that the principal is truly interested in student issues and concerns.

Unmotivated Students

Characteristics:

These are students who may be excessively:

- disorganized
- forgetful
- dawdling
- not completing assignments
- lonely
- withdrawn
- whining/complaining
- bossy

- aggressive
- hyperactive
- passive
- perfectionist
- dramatic
- socially isolated
- rebellious
- ill

Underlying Causes:

These students may:

1. Have families in which:
   - expectations are too high, or too low
   - parents are overly demanding, or permissive
   - parents are overly neglectful, or protective
   - conflict is intense and/or frequent
   - criticism is frequent
   - sibling rivalry is intense

2. Have a classroom environment that is:
   - not sensitive enough to the student's
     - learning styles
     - learning modalities
     - feelings and beliefs
     - culture and/or ethnicity
     - developmental levels
   - not flexible enough
   - not relevant enough to the student's world
   - not invitational enough socially, emotionally, and/or academically
   - overly demanding, or permissive
   - overprotective
   - overly competitive

Strategies:

1. Ensure that each of these children is emotionally connected with an adult (e.g., parent or mentor) and a peer who are supportive of the value of the child's schoolwork, and social and emotional welfare.

2. Emphasize that the child is liked for who he/she is, not because of school success.

3. Involve the child in more cooperative learning, team projects, and paired activities rather than individual work.

4. Be supportive and avoid blaming, lecturing, or preaching to the child about schoolwork, but emphasize that it is his or her responsibility.

5. Help these children work with interactive skills and separation anxiety.

6. Encourage parents to be supportive, but not too restrictive with schoolwork times.

7. Be accepting and encouraging. Place a strip of masking tape over the child's desk. Every time the child is paying attention, ask or cue him to make a check mark. Later, send a note home stating how many checks he received. The same thing will work with parents with tape on a refrigerator, or space on a wall in the house.

8. Set realistic goals for the child.

9. Teach and model active learning and problem solving.

10. Reward interest in learning and actual academic achievements.

11. Have a powerful incentive system.

12. Teach effective motivational strategies
    A. Teach self-control
    B. Change the way children look at themselves by:
       • providing feedback rewards.
       • helping child to look at "achievers."
       • changing child's self image to one of success and responsibility.
       • encouraging positive self-talk.

13. Influence school to be more motivational.

14. Do not emphasize or share individual grades.

15. Do not publicly criticize student's poor work.

16. Do not announce that a student who usually does poorly did well.

17. Do not compare papers or children.

18. Teach children to deal with losing.

19. Involve the student in planning and determining assignments, setting goals, and self-assessment. Encourage student to "PACE" themselves:

P Practice success. Make sure the student has opportunities to succeed many times during the day.

A Actively involve students in planning or determining assignments, setting goals, and self-assessment.

C Change visual, auditory, or affective perceptions of him or herself. Change the method of instruction to use a variety of teaching strategies. Communicate to the child that you value him.

E Encourage students frequently by praise or rewards.

20. Share the following strategies with parents:
    - Model positive attitudes toward achievement.
    - Don't complain about spouse's overwork or say bad things about the other's career.
    - Provide definite limits.
    - Give clear, consistent messages toward achievement.
    - Avoid giving "yes-no" messages where unpleasant consequences merge with pleasant ones.
    - Teach organization and involvement in household chores.
    - Avoid nagging.
    - Encourage homework study to be quiet, alone and at a desk or table. Do not sit beside child during this time.
    - Avoid talking about how you also "hated" school or didn't do well without balancing this with how you "turned things around." This could enhance child identification with parent and encourage underachievement.
    - Be aware of own patterns and tendencies toward procrastination, passive, aggressive behavior.
    - Maintain power over child in discipline as opposed to child being more powerful or in control of parents and teachers.
    - Avoid complaining too much about work - may lead to children complaining about their work/school.
    - Parents should resist the temptation to impose their fantasies on your child. Allow them to establish their own goals.
    - Beware of equating excessive achievement with happiness.

People Become Motivated
When Their Basic Needs Are Met . . .

According to William Glasser, "To understand what motivation is, it is necessary first to understand that control theory contends that all human beings are born with five basic needs built into their genetic structure: survival, love, power, fun, and freedom. All of our lives we must attempt to live in a way that will best satisfy one or more of these needs."

Besides survival, our basic needs are:
Love - belonging, friendship, caring, involvement
Power - importance, recognition, skill, competence
Fun - pleasure, enjoyment, learning, laughter
Freedom - choice, independence, liberty, autonomy

Take a few minutes to complete the chart below. Are your basic needs being met in your personal life and in your present occupation or work setting? Are you trying to help your students meet their basic needs in your classroom?

	What are you presently doing in your personal life to meet these basic needs?	Are your basic needs being met in your present work setting? How?	List ways in which you are helping your students meet their needs in your classroom.
Love			
Power			
Fun			
Freedom			

"Circle of Friends"

PURPOSE:

To make adolescents aware of how peers influence their choice of friends.

To allow students to compare what qualities they consider important in friends to the people they spend most of their time with.

This activity teaches students the effect certain people can have on them.

PROCEDURE:

Have students draw on both sides of a standard size piece of paper a circle (about the size of a nickel) and write ME in the center. Then have students draw a circle around the middle circle (large enough to write several things inside of it). Then have students draw a third circle outside that one. On one side of the paper, next to the ME, have students write several words that describe what a very close friend is to them. Then have students write, in the inner circle, the characteristics of so-so friends. Lastly, on the outside of the circle ask students to write characteristics of an acquaintance.

Now have students turn their paper over to the opposite side. Ask them to think of the names of the people who they spend most of their time with. Have them write their names in the inside circle closest to the ME. Then have them think of the names of the people they spend some time with, on weekends or going to social events, etc. Then, have them write the names of several people who they only pass in the hall or see in the lunch room or just occasionally see.

FOLLOW UP:

Have students compare their idea of a close friend to who they spend most of their time with. Then, the names of those they spend some of their time with compared to their definition of so-so friends. And those they see very little compared to their definition of an acquaintance. Ask students if those particular people possess those qualities they described for that category of friends.

Ask them to look at what kind of people they spend most of their time with. Are they the kinds of friends they want to spend most of their time with?

"Secret Admirer"

PROCEDURE:

Have students draw a picture of a person or character who they would most want to be like.

Then ask them to share their drawing in a small group and tell why they chose this person. Ask them to describe the qualities they like most about that person or character.

FOLLOW UP:

Have students share what qualities they wish they had like the person they described. Have students discuss which qualities were realistic ones for them and how they could set a goal to make this change.

Students could also talk about what positive qualities they possess and how they each have at least one thing they can do well.

"Down In The Dumps"

PROCEDURE:

Motivation

Talk about feeling "down in the dumps." Point out that it is normal for teenager and preteens to experience low moods and confusing mood swings. Ask class members what makes them feel down in the dumps.

Activity

1. Distribute the Activity Sheet: *Down in the Dumps* and have students complete it individually.

2. Put students into small groups. Have them use the Activity Sheets to plan a role-playing exercise that shows someone who's feeling "down in the dumps." Ask several or all groups to present these skills to the class.

3. Tell each group to plan a second skit in which the person overcomes his/her unhappy feelings. Ask several or all groups to present these skits to the class.

WRAP-UP:

Ask each group for additional suggestions for overcoming feelings of depression. Discuss what everyone can do when they are around someone who is "down in the dumps."

Down In The Dumps

Directions: Answer the questions below.

1. What makes one feel down in the dumps?
   Give an example.

2. Do your friends understand when you are in a bad mood?
   Give an example.

3 What effect does your mood have on those around you?
   Give an example.

4. What are some things you can do to get back in a good mood?
   Give an example.

5. When you're in a bad mood, do you sometimes do things you wouldn't normally do - such as misbehave in class or talk disrespectfully to others? Give an example.

With your group:

• Plan a role-playing skit about being "down in the dumps."

• Plan a second skit in which the person overcomes his/her bad feelings.

• Be prepared to present these skits in front of the class.

Highlights of Research on Strategies for Motivating Students to Learn

Research on student motivation to learn indicate promising principles suitable for application in classrooms, summarized here for quick reference.

Essential Preconditions

1. Supportive environment.
2. Appropriate level of challenge/difficulty.
3. Meaningful learning objectives.
4. Moderation/optimal use.

Motivating by Maintaining Success Expectations

5. Program for success.
6. Teach goal setting, performance appraisal, and self-reinforcement.
7. Help students to recognize linkages between effort and outcome.
8. Provide remedial socialization.

Motivating by Supplying Extrinsic Incentives

9. Offer rewards for good (or improved) performance.
10. Structure appropriate competition.
11. Call attention to the instrumental value of academic activities.

Motivating by Capitalizing on Students' Intrinsic Motivation

12. Adapt tasks to students' interests.
13. Include novelty/variety elements.
14. Allow opportunities to make choices or autonomous decisions.
15. Provide opportunities for students to respond actively.
16. Provide immediate feedback to student responses.
17. Allow students to create finished products.
18. Include fantasy or simulation elements.
19. Incorporate game-like features.
20. Include higher-level objectives and divergent questions.
21. Provide opportunities to interact with peers.

Stimulating Student Motivation to Learn

22. Model interest in learning and motivation to learn.
23. Communicate desirable expectations and attributions about students' motivation to learn.
24. Minimize students' performance anxieties during learning activities.
25. Project intensity.
26. Project enthusiasm.
27. Induce task interest or appreciation.
28. Induce curiosity or suspense.

29. Induce dissonance or cognitive conflict.
30. Make abstract content more personal, concrete, or familiar.
31. Induce students to generate their own motivation to learn.
32. State learning objectives and provide advance organizers.
33. Model task-related thinking and problem solving.

Source: Brophy, 1987: "Synthesis of Research on Strategies for Motivating Students to Learn." Educational Leadership, 45(2). p.45. Copyright 1987 by the Association for Supervision and Curriculum Development.

Underachievement Checklist

CODE: 0=NEVER, 1=SOMETIMES 2=OFTEN, 3=ALWAYS

_____1.   My child's schoolwork is sloppy and illegible.

_____ 2.   My child's projects are often incomplete.

_____ 3.   My child procrastinates.

_____ 4.   My child is having difficulty keeping up with his or her classwork.

_____ 5.   My child's work is not handed in on time.

_____ 6.   My child is disorganized at home.

_____ 7.   My child is disorganized at school.

_____ 8.   My child is irresponsible.

_____ 9.   My child is forgetful.

_____10.   My child lacks pride in his or her work.

_____ 11.   My child shows little motivation.

_____ 12.   My child avoids academic work.

_____ 13.   My child makes excuses for poor performance.

_____ 14.   My child avoids challenges.

_____ 15.   My child lacks self-confidence.

_____ 16.   My child becomes easily discouraged.

_____ 17.   My child abandons difficult projects.

_____ 18.   My child is easily frustrated.

_____ 19.   My child appears to be functioning below his or her potential.

Interpreting the Checklist

SCORE

0-2 Your child is not manifesting symptoms of underachievement.

3-7 Your child is manifesting subtle symptoms of potential underachievement. His or her school performance should be monitored.

8-20 Your child is manifesting moderate symptoms of underachievement and perhaps a learning problem. This range of scores should be considered a danger signal. Your child's school performance should be very closely monitored.

21-57 Your child is manifesting significant symptoms of either underachievement or a specific learning disability. he/she is at risk academically and emotionally, and active intervention is recommended. You should request that your child be evaluated by the school psychologist.

From: Greene, L.J. <u>Kids Who Underachieve.</u> New York: Simon and Schuster, 1986.

Ten Gifts
That Will Help Students
Feel More Positive About Themselves

Give them *responsibility*.

Give them a *part in decision-making*.

Give them *permission for their feelings*.

Give them *reasonable rules*.

Give them *"guard rails."*

Give them *unconditional hugs*.

Give them *permission to make mistakes*.

Give them *the truth*.

Give them *freedom*.

Give them *themselves*.

Ways To Say,
"Good for You!"

I bet your mom and dad would be proud to see the job you did on this.
Thank you for (sitting down, being quiet, getting right to work, etc.)
Thank you for raising your hand, Charles. What is it?
It's a pleasure to teach when you work like this.
I like the way Bill (the class) has settled down.
I'm proud of the way you worked (are working) today.
That looks like it's going to be a great report.
It looks like you put a lot of work into this.
That's an interesting way of looking at it.
Please show it to the class.
This kind of work pleases me very much.
Congratulations! You only missed _____.
Sherri is really going to town.
I like the way you are working.
You really outdid yourself today.
That's right. Good for you.
I like the way Tom is working.
My goodness, how impressive.
You're on the right track now.
Now you've got the hang of it.
That's a very good observation.
That's coming along nicely.
That's quite an improvement.
Everyone's working so hard.
I appreciate your help.
Ann is paying attention.
Now you've figured it out.
That's the right answer.
You make it look easy.
Thank you very much.
Keep up the good work.
That's a good point.
You've got it now.
What neat work.
Excellent work.
Very interesting.
Very creative.
That's clever.
Nice going.
That's great.

Source: Unknown

Famous People Who
Survived "Difficult Times"
(And Later Achieved Fame Through Excellence)

Louisa May Alcott was told by an editor that she could never write anything that had popular appeal.

Ann Bancroft, a polar explorer, struggled with dyslexia in school, yet in 1986 became the first woman to reach the North Pole.

Beethoven's music teacher once said of him, "as a composer he is hopeless."

Admiral Richard E. Byrd had been retired from the Navy as "unfit for service" until he flew over both Poles.

Caruso's music teacher told him, "You can't sing. You have no voice at all."

George Washington Carver was born a slave. When he was an infant, his mother was sold and shipped away. He later held three patents that revolutionized agriculture.

Agatha Christie had a writing disability so severe that she had to dictate her mystery novels for others to type.

Winston Churchill failed the first form (grade) school.

Bill Cosby dropped out of high school. He later received his doctorate in Education and became one of the most successful entertainers and businessmen in the United states.

A newspaper fired **Walt Disney** because he had "no good ideas."

When **Thomas Edison** was a boy, his teachers told him he was too stupid to learn anything. He made 3,000 mistakes on his way to inventing the light bulb. Eventually he held 1,093 patents.

Einstein was four years old before he could speak, and seven before he could read.

The director of the Imperial Opera in Vienna told **Madam Schumann-Heink** that she would never be a singer and advised her to buy a sewing machine.

Michael Jordan was cut from his high school basketball team.

B. B. King lived in poverty as a child and worked in the cotton fields. He became one of the most successful musicians in the history of the blues.

Abraham Lincoln entered the Black Hawk War as a captain and came out as a private and still became President of the United States.

Isaac Newton did poorly in grade school.

Louis Pasteur was rated as "mediocre" in chemistry when he attended Royal College.

Wilma Rudolph contracted polio and scarlet fever as a child, and wore leg braces for nine years. She eventually became the first woman from the United States to win three gold medals in track and field in the Olympics.

Leo Tolstoy flunked out of college.

Wernher Von Braun flunked ninth grade algebra.

Fred Waring was once rejected for high school chorus.

Oprah Winfrey suffered sexual abuse in her past, yet she became the first black women to host a nationally syndicated weekday talk show and to own her own television and film production company.

F. W. Woolworth got a job in a dry goods store when he was 21, but his employers would not let him wait on a customer because he "didn't have enough sense."

Summary

What did these people all have in common, in addition to great ability? They took great risks. They took chances again and again. They took their failures in stride and kept on trying. They liked being challenged. They made mistakes and learned from them. You can, too.

"He who never made a mistake never made a discovery."   -**Samuel Smiles**

Daydreamers

Daydreaming or fantasizing is important in our lives. Effective decision-making and problem-solving require some dreaming to ensure creativity in the process. Daydreaming can help us to think of new goals for ourselves, and rehearse ways to reach those goals in the safety of our minds.

Daydreaming is also an important part of the psychological healing process. It helps us to consciously begin to deal with grief, loss, fear, and anger. However, daydreaming can become problematic when the intensity, frequency or duration of the behavior begins to interfere with learning.

Characteristics:

These students may be:
- pleasant
- wishful
- imaginative
- escape prone
- creative
- distracted

Underlying Causes:

1. Daydreaming is often an escape from fear, sadness, or anger.

2. Day dreaming may be a critical part of psychological healing.

3. Daydreaming may be a compensation for real disabilities.

4. Daydreaming may be a habit.

5. Daydreaming may help a child feel more powerful.

6. Children may be seeking solutions or a deeper understanding of problems.

7. Daydreaming may be the result of a physical cause such as:
   - brain dysfunction
   - medication
   - illness or allergies
   - lack of sleep
   - substance abuse

Strategies:

1. Plan exciting, busy activities so that the child will have less opportunity to daydream. Real life must become as interesting as daydreaming.

2. Reward attentiveness and productivity in both tangible and intangible ways.

3. Provide some brief "down times" during the day when it is okay for children to let their minds "wander."

4. Assess the theme of daydreaming.
    Possible themes of daydreamers and activities to deal with.
    A few common themes include:
    *   Divorce
    *   Alcoholism
    *   Physical and/or emotional abuse
    *   Loss
    *   Shyness
    *   Lack of friends
    *   Lack of nurturing at home

5. Write a contract specifying what is expected.

6. Talk with parents.

7. Avoid competition initially as it may cause child to be uninterested.

8. Tap into what the student enjoys doing.

9. Investigate the possibility of drug or alcohol abuse.

10. Help children see the difference between reality and fantasy.

11. Help "Day Dreamers" utilize their imagination to bring about positive self-change.

12. Do not be overly critical, demanding, or abrupt to a child who is daydreaming. Bring the student back to task with a gentle touch, or statement.

"Beat the Clock"

PROCEDURE:

Set a timer for a reasonable amount of time in which to complete the task.

Suggest that the child work to beat the clock, and if they do, they could earn one chip (or other token), lunch with the principal, or to be "Principal for the Day."

FOLLOW UP:

Have students discuss:

- Feelings about "beating the clock."

- The amount and quality of work that they completed.

- Their plans for the next time they work on a task like this. Do they need the same time, more time, or less time?

"Dream Collage"

PURPOSE:

To give students an opportunity to express their daydreams.

To talk about concerns, dreams, or wishes students may have.

To talk about ways students might set goals and reach their dreams.

To problem solve ways students may cope with and/or resolve some of their concerns.

PROCEDURE:

1. Ask students to draw a picture of themselves or write their name in the center of a sheet of construction paper.

2. Ask each student to cut out and paste pictures, words, and phrases that describe their daydreams.

3. Have students share the finished products in pairs, or in small groups.

FOLLOW UP:

Ask students to share with their partner(s) if their daydreams are primarily about concerns or worries, or about goals. Then ask them to brainstorm together if they have any supportive ideas for each other.

Lead a discussion about when daydreams can be helpful and important, and when they might interfere with important tasks such as taking a test, paying attention in class, or listening to a friend.

Have students share ideas about how to set time aside to daydream, and how to stop daydreaming when it might interfere with other important tasks.

Section VII

Special Bonus Section:

Trends in the Home

compiled by:

Tom Carr

Abuse and Violence
in the Home

- Of 339 cases of physical abuse reported to Iowa's Department of Human Services by non-parents, such as teachers or counselors, 290 were caused by boyfriends. (McManus, 1993)

- "The home is actually a more dangerous place for women than the city streets. Each day, four women are killed by their male partners."

- 99% of kidnappers and the large majority of physical and sexual abusers of children are their parents. (USA TODAY, 5-3-90)

- An estimated 1,200 children die each year from child abuse or neglect; those who survive are often damaged for life. The experience of physical abuse as a child, for example, increases the risk of chronic aggressive behavior by almost 300%. (New York Times, 12-21-90)

- Neglect is the type of child maltreatment most strongly correlated with poverty, incest the least; but economic stress, material deprivation, social isolation, and educational deficits, such as unrealistic expectations of children's capacities - all closely associated with poverty - substantially increase the chance that maltreatment will occur. (Pelton, 1978)

- One study in Wisconsin found that cases of child abuse increased by an average of 123% in counties where the unemployment rate had risen 3.1% or more; counties in which unemployment declined had reduced reports of abuse. (Coontz, 1992)

- 92% of the victims of child sexual abuse are girls; 97% of the abusers are male. Incest tends to occur in families with strong patterns of paternal dominance and authoritarianism, along with values reinforcing the submission of women and children. (Coontz, 1992)

- In a recent survey of 1,000 U.S. adults sponsored by the Family Violence Prevention Fund, found: 14% of the women say they have been beaten by a husband or boyfriend, 34% say they've witnessed domestic violence. (USA TODAY, 4-20-93)

- In this country, a woman is beaten every 18 seconds. Every year, some three million women are smacked, hit, punched, kicked, stomped, scalded, burned, stabbed, shot, mutilated, or sexually tortured by the men who say they love them. Four women a day are killed, many of them after they had left their abusers. (Foley and Nechas, 1993)

- Battered women are seen in emergency rooms more frequently than patients with appendicitis. In one hospital, 70% of the victims of violence are battered women. (Foley and Nechas, 1993)

- "The most important source of violence by and among children is family breakdown. More that 60% of children born today will spend at least some time in a single-parent household before reaching age 18."

- Researchers at the University of Maryland School of Medicine in Baltimore recently completed a study of 168 teenagers who visited an inner-city clinic for routine medical care. The teens were questioned about their exposure to various kinds of violence. A stunning 24% had witnessed a murder and 72% know someone who had been shot. (Zinsmeister, 1990)

- In a recent newspaper article Arthur Caplan, director of the center for Biomedical Ethics at the University of Minnesota Medical School, noted: The FBI reports that a woman is beaten every 12 seconds in this country. The American Medical Association estimates that nearly a third of the women seen in emergency rooms are victims of domestic violence. The National Council of Juvenile and Family Court Judges says that more than half the men who batter their wives also abuse their children. Government surveys show that domestic violence was responsible for more than 100,000 hospital days, 30,000 emergency room visits, and 40,000 visits to the doctor each year. (Knight-Ridder, 6-24-93)

Children and Television

- American teenagers spend, on average, about twenty-one hours per week watching television. By contrast, they read for pleasure about 1.8 hours per week and spend 5.6 hours on homework. (Nat'l Center Education Stats. 1990)

- One study found that eleven and twelve-year-old boys watch television an average of twenty-six hours per week. (Timmer, Eccles, O'Brien, 1985)

- Television viewing peaks at around age twelve and declines through later teen years. It may represent the only activity some children share with parents or siblings. (Carnegie Corp. 1992)

- A study commissioned by TV GUIDE reported that in a single day, TV showed 1,846 acts of violence, 389 assaults, 362 gunplay, and 273 punches. (NBC Nightly News, 5-21-93)

- Dr. Branden Centerwell, an epidemiologist at the University of Washington, in a recent study showed that the white homicide rate in the United States increased 93% between the introduction of TV in 1945 and 1974. In South Africa, which had no TV until 1974, it declined 7% during the same period. (USA TODAY, 6-8-93)

- According to Nielson data, by age eighteen, the average American child will have watched 22,000 hours of television. That's double the 11,000 hours spent in school. (McManus, 1993)

- Dr. Brandon Centerwell, an expert on media violence, writes: "TV is a factor in 10,000 homicides each year." (McManus, 1993)

- Dr. Tom Radecki, a psychiatrist who created the National Coalition on Television Violence, says that entertainment violence is responsible for 25-50% of all domestic violence in the United States. He cites studies that show that kids with a heavy TV diet are more likely to solve problems with peers by punching them. Long-term studies show that heavy TV watchers are more likely to become pregnant while unmarried, delinquent as teenagers, and criminal as adults. (McManus, 1993)

- The movie "Robocop 2," starring Arnold Schwarzenegger, has 147 violent acts per hour. (McManus, 1993)

- A study begun on a group of eight-year-olds by Leonard Eron and Rowell Huesmann of the University of Illinois tried to identify all causes of aggression in childhood: child-rearing practices in the family, neighborhood experiences, and other factors. At the end of the ten years, the single best predictor of violence in these children, now 18, was what they had watched on television when they were eight years old - not what their families did, not what their social class was, not any of the other things that were measured. (Education Week, 10-4-89)

- Recent research generally identifies three problems connected with TV violence: Children may become less sensitive to the pain and suffering of others; they may be more likely to behave in aggressive or harmful ways toward others. (Education Week, 10-4-89)

- Columnist George Will tells of a study done in a remote Canadian community that first had television in 1973. Before television was introduced, the researchers monitored rates of inappropriate aggression among 45 first and second-graders. After two years of television, the rate of aggression increased 160%, in both boys and girls, and in both those who were aggressive to begin with and those who were not. Other researchers studied third, fourth, and fifth grade boys in two Indian communities in northern Manitoba. One got television in 1973, the other in 1977. The aggressiveness of boys in the first community increased immediately, in the second it increased four years later. (Will, 1993)

- "Next to parents, television is, perhaps, a child's most influential teacher." (Boyer, 1991)

- The amount of time children spend watching television is awesome. A six-month-old, peering through the rails of a crib, views television, on average, about one and a half hours every day. A five year-old watches an hour a day more. By the time the child sets foot in kindergarten, he/she is likely to have spent more than four thousand hours in front of this electronic teacher. (Liebert and Sprafkin, 1988)

- On Saturday morning, during the so-called "children's hour," youngsters are served a steady diet of junk-food commercials and cartoons that contain, on average, twenty-six acts of violence every six minutes. (Radecki, 1991)

- According to a Harvard University study, 70% of today's parents feel that children are watching too much television. Although 40% of parents believe that such viewing has a negative effect on their kids, pediatricians at the University of California found that barely 15% of the parents guide their children in selecting programs. Two-thirds do not frequently discuss program content with their children, and 66 % often use television to entertain. (Taras, 1990) served a steady diet of junk-food commercials and cartoons that contain, on average, twenty-six acts of violence every six minutes. (Radecki, 1991)

Health Issues

- For the past 20 years, government and scholarly estimates of the number of children 18 and under who suffer from mental disorders have hovered around 12% of that population. But a recent report from the Institute of Sciences suggests that figure may actually be as high as 17-22% - 11 million to 14 million children. (The Atlantic, June 1991)

- The suicide rate for white adolescent males has tripled in the past thirty years, as has that of all young people 15-24. (The Atlantic, June 1991)

- "The day-to-day physical nourishment of babies - the quality of care they get during the first months and years of life - will shape profoundly their readiness for school. If there is one right that every child can claim, it is the right to a healthy start." (Boyer, 1991)

- Raising our expectations for educational performance will not produce the needed improvement unless we also reduce the barriers to learning that are represented by poor student health. (Boyer, 1991)

- Mothers who smoke during pregnancy place their child at risk for low birthweight, asthma, and growth retardation. The effects of smoking are cumulative, with children of heavy smokers scoring lower on verbal tests than those of lighter smokers or non-smokers. (Newman and Buka, 1990)

- Approximately forty thousand babies are born each year in this country with serious problems directly related to alcohol abuse by mothers during pregnancy. About 7,000 of them have fetal-alcohol syndrome, a condition that results in mental retardation. Another 33,000 have learning problems, limited attention span, speech and language deficiencies, and hyperactivity. (Newman and Buka, 1990)

- More that 10% of all newborns in the U.S. - 425,000 in 1988 - had mothers who used marijuana, cocaine, crack, heroin, or amphetamines during pregnancy. Cocaine and crack are associated with prematurity, smaller head circumference, and lower birthweight, all of which place a child educationally at risk. (Boyer, 1991)

- In a Carnegie Foundation survey of teachers, more than half of the respondents said that, "poor nourishment" among students is a problem at their school. 60% cited "poor health" as a problem. (Boyer, 1991)

- For every alcoholic, it is estimated that four or five family members and friends, 35-45 million persons, are directly affected by the disease. (Wilson and Blocher, 1990)

- Children of alcoholics often have school and/or behavior problems, characterized by fighting with peers, temper tantrums, disruptive classroom behavior, poor academic performance, truancy, delinquency, and/or abuse of alcohol and other drugs. (Wilson and Blocher, 1990)

- Children of alcoholics account for some 20% of all referrals to child guidance clinics and approximately 40-90% of case loads in child and family agencies. (Woodside, 1982)

- Eating disorders, which are found most frequently in middle-class female adolescents, have been increasing in prevalence over the past few years. In fact, anorexia nervosa and bulimia are estimated to occur in 5-10% of adolescent girls and young women. (Nassar, Hodges, Ollendick, 1992)

- Data indicate that one out of every six children will lose one parent by death before his or her eighteenth birthday. These losses affect the child's behavior and performance in school. Students often miss classes, do not complete assignments, do poorer quality work, exhibit rebellious behavior, or withdraw into depression. (Glass, 1991)

- The Children's Defense Fund noted the following:
  - In 1989, 20,000 babies were born to mothers who did not receive timely, adequate prenatal care.
  - 10.7 million children younger than 18 (in 1988) were completely uninsured.
  - The poorest children ages 5-17 lose 1.5 times more days of school because of acute or chronic health conditions.
  - Every 64 seconds an infant is born to a teenage mother. Every five minutes an infant is born to a teenage mother who already had a child.
  (Children's Defense Fund, 1991 Report)

- Figures for 1990 show AIDS killed more men ages 25-44 than accidents, homicide, heart disease or cancer in 64 major cities and in the states of New York, New Jersey, California, Florida, and Massachusetts.

- In 1992, 1330 eighth graders in North Carolina were surveyed about their biggest worries, fears, and concerns. Four of their top ten worries had to do with death, dying, and health related issues:

Rank	Worry, Fear, or Concerns
1	Getting good grades
2	Their parents' health
3	Friend, relative, family member dying
4	Taking tests
5	Getting into college
6	Getting a good job after high school/college
7	Not being attractive
8	Dying
9	Going to high school
10	Getting AIDS

(Carr, 1992)

- The prevalence for depression in children up to the age of 12, drawn from the general population, ranges from 2% (major depression) to about 15% (moderate depression). (Hopper and Christensen, 1991)

- Prevalence of Attention Deficit Disorder within the U.S. school-age population could conservatively be estimated to be between 3-5%. Boys are four to nine times more likely than girls to have ADD. (Parker, 1992)

- The incidence of learning problems and underachievement within the population of children with ADD was once estimated from 43% to 92%. (Parker, 1992)

- In terms of behavior, ADD children have a greater likelihood than other children of having behavior disorders. It is estimated that between 40 and 60% of children with ADD will show signs of co-existing oppositional defiant disorder (ODD). Half of those children, in turn, will develop a conduct disorder (CD). (Parker, 1992)

Parenting in the 90's

- In a recent Gallup Poll most modern mothers think they are doing a better job of communicating with their children (though a worse job of house cleaning) than did their own mothers and they put a higher value on spending time with their family than did their mothers.

- In a recent poll, 71% of the respondents said they were "very satisfied" with their own family life, but more than half rated the overall quality of family life as negative; "I'm okay; you're not."

- Many authorities argue that highly aggressive, violent children are more likely to come from punitive, authoritarian families, especially abusive ones, rather than permissive ones. (Coontz, 1992)

- There is evidence that "full-time" housewives are more likely than working mothers to use violence against their children. (Coontz, 1992)

- Sons of working mothers appear to have more respect for women than do other boys and are more likely to see men as warm and expressive. (Coontz, 1992)

- In one study, the families of rapists were far more likely than those of non-rapists to contain wives who were full-time homemakers. (Coontz, 1992)

- "When children are socially and emotionally supported by caring adults, their prospects for learning are wonderfully enhanced. If, however, children are denied this supportive home environment during the first years of life, it will be more difficult for them to succeed fully in school." (Boyer, 1991)

- "The vast numbers of children today grow up in environments that are language poor." (Boyer, 1991)

- According to one survey, parents talk to their children, on average, just a few minutes a day, usually giving orders. (Boyer, 1991)

- A U.S. Department of Education report recently revealed that nearly 30% of today's parents do not regularly read aloud to their children and nearly 60% don't tell their children stories. (Boyer, 1991)

- The arts are an essential part of language which must be developed if school readiness is to be achieved. Yet, according to a recent survey, only 39% of parents regularly engage in music activities with their children. Only one-third engage in arts and craft activities. (Boyer, 1991)

- The Carnegie Foundation surveyed five thousand fifth and eighth graders. They found that, "60% said they wish they could spend more time with their mothers and fathers. Nearly one-third said their families never sit down to eat a meal together." (Boyer, 1991)

- According to a Louis Harris survey, half of the nation's adults feel that the quality of family life in this country has deteriorated. Three out of four say that problems affecting children today are worse than when they were growing up. 60% confirm that it is difficult to find enough time for their children. (Boyer, 1991)

- A recent survey compared methods of discipline that parents favor today and these methods were compared to those favored by parents 30 years ago.

- Methods of discipline favored by parents: 1962 and 1992:

Type of discipline	1962	1992
Time-out	20%	38%
Lecture them in a nice way	23%	24%
Spanking	59%	19%
Take away TV privileges	38%	15%
Scold (not in a nice way)	17%	15%
"Ground" them	5%	14%
Take away allowance	4%	2%

  *Note: parents could cite more than one method   (Bruskin-Goldring Research, 1993)

- One survey of 1,000 adolescents found that they spend an average of five minutes a day exclusively with their fathers and about twenty minutes with their mothers. (Csikszentmihalyi and Larson, 1984)

- Eva Margolis and Louis Genevie interviewed 1,100 mothers of all ages and published the results in their books, *The Motherhood Report, How Women Feel About Being Mothers*. Highlights from the study include:
  - Only one in four mothers had very positive feelings about motherhood.
  - One in five views motherhood in a very negative way.
  - Many mothers with children under 12 said infancy was their least favorite stage of motherhood.
  - Twice as many women said their marriages took a turn for the worse after they had children. (Foley and Nechas, 1993)

- Attention is important between marriage partners, but it is fundamental for children. Infants who do not get enough attention, in the sense of psychic interaction and love, simply cannot survive, even if they are fed and clothed. In a study in Chicago it was found that the children of "warm families" (families where high levels of attention were given to each member) were significantly different from children of "cool families" (families where parents are distracted and inattentive and did not relate well to each other). Children of warm homes are more sympathetic, helpful, caring, and supporting. Warm homes also breed children who are less denying, defensive, and unsure of their worth. (Csikszentmihalyi, 1981)

- The book, *New Families, No Families* takes a close look at household chores in the 1990's. Highlights include:
  - Children are helping less around the house than in the past.
  - Educated parents are less likely to require them to help.
  - As a mother's education level rises, the work asked of her children declines.
  - Husbands in highly educated households contribute significantly more than those in less educated families.
  - Women continue to bear the overwhelming burden for keeping the household running.
  - Husbands in highly educated households may be taking up the share of work previously done by children.
  - Husbands are making a greater contribution in households where the mother works more hours and earns more money.
  - There has been a decline in the amount of time spent on housework overall.
  - Women are more aware of the work they do and may not realize all that their husbands are doing, and vice versa.
  - Growing up in a female-headed household results in greater participation in household chores among children than growing up in an intact family, so much that boys in mother-only families are more involved in household tasks than girls in two-parent families. (Goldscheider and White, 1991)

In the book, *Secrets of Strong Families*, the authors headed up research done on 3,000 families. Results from their studies showed that the top six factors that go into the making of a strong family are (in rank order):
1. Commitment
2. Appreciation of family members
3. Communication
4. Time together
5. Spiritual wellness
6. Ability to cope with stress and crisis
   (Stinnitt and Defrain, 1986)

- Therapist John Bradshaw explains away this generation's problems with the dictum that 96% of families are dysfunctional, made that way by the addicted society we live in. (Whitehead, 1993)

- America's young adolescents have a great deal of discretionary time. Much of it is unstructured, unsupervised, and unproductive. Only 60% of adolescents' waking hours are committed to such essentials as school, homework, eating, chores, or paid employment, while fully 40% is discretionary. (Carnegie Report, 1992)

- A recent survey of 25,000 eighth graders found that 27% of the respondents regularly spent two or more hours home alone after school. Eighth graders from families in the lowest socioeconomic group were more likely to report that they are home alone for more than three hours a day. (Carnegie Report, 1992)

- 70% of women with children under the age of five work full-time. (Brazelton, 1993)

- There has been much research lately on parenting styles (permission, authoritarian, and authoritative/democratic). Time after time, research shows that children reared in authoritative or democratic homes are more likely to be successful in school (better grades and less behavior problems) than children raised in permissive or authoritarian homes. Best estimates are that only 25-30% of homes in the U.S. are authoritative or democratic. (Carr, 1992)

- 152 fourth and fifth graders at an elementary school in Hillsborough, North Carolina were surveyed. The results of the survey revealed that the more successful students had a much more positive perception of their non-school hours. Listed below in rank order are the five areas that the more successful students perceived in a much more favorable way than did the less successful students:
  1. They perceived their families spent much more quality time together.
  2. They believed they had good behavior at home.
  3. They had higher levels of self-esteem.
  4. Their parents were more consistent with following through with stated consequences.
  5. They had no doubts about their parents' love for them.
  (Carr, 1993)

Marriage and Divorce

- According to polls by George Gallup, what sparked three-fifths of divorces was simply poor communication. (McManus, 1993)

- Half of all newlyweds will divorce. Another tenth will permanently separate. That's a 60% dissolution rate! (McManus, 1993)

- The divorce rate in Europe is half that of the United States. (McManus, 1993)

- Second marriages are just as likely to fail as first marriages. Second marriages that break apart do so more quickly - about six years for a second divorce, after an initial median marriage of eight years. (McManus, 1993)

- About 40% of children will see parents divorce by age eight, and half will see a second pair of parents divorce by age eighteen. (McManus, 1993)

- Research studies show that divorce and the process of marital breakup puts people at a much higher risk for both psychiatric and physical disease, even cancer. (McManus, 1993)

- Research by J.J. Lynch reveals that divorced men are twice as likely to die from heart disease, stroke, hypertension, and cancer as married men in any given year. And death for the divorced is four times more likely via auto accidents and suicide; seven times higher for cirrhosis of the liver and pneumonia; eightfold greater by murder, and psychiatric illness is ten times more likely. (McManus, 1993)

- Larson studied 20,000 white women and found that married women are far less prone to physical illness than are single women who suffer more chronic conditions and spent more days in bed than did married women. For example, divorced women's odds of dying in a given year from cancer of the mouth, digestive organs, lungs, and breast are two to three times that of married women. (McManus, 1993)

- According to the Gallup Poll, only 17% of marriages break up because of adultery. But 47% end because of "incompatibility." (McManus, 1993)

- According to a National Survey of Family Growth sponsored by the National Institute of Child Development, "Those who were active in practicing their faith are more than twice as likely to stay married as the non-religious." (McManus, 1993)

- Psychology Today reported in its July/August 1988 issues about a Swedish study. Yale University sociologist Neil Bennett and colleagues found that cohabiting women were 80% more likely to separate or divorce than were women who had not lived with their spouses before marriage. (McManus, 1993)

- The National Survey of Families and Households reported in 1989: "Unions begun by cohabitation are almost twice as likely to dissolve within ten years compared to all first marriages." (McManus, 1993)

- "Have you ever wondered why the divorce rate in Japan is about one-fourth that in the United States? Perhaps one reason is that Japanese choose partners who will be approved by their families, while American couples choose their marriage partners without any regard for family approval. Apparently, the Japanese families have a clearer vision for who is a suitable partner for a child than the adult child has on his own!" (McManus, 1993)

- Of the 1,183,000 U.S. marriages that ended in divorce in 1988, the median length of those that dissolved was seven years. (McManus, 1993)

- Three-fifths of marriages failed due to poor communication, or to poor conflict-resolution skills. (McManus, 1993)

- One Gallup Poll reported in 1989, "In an era of increasingly fragile marriages, a couple's ability to communicate is the single most important contributor to a stable and satisfying marriage." (McManus, 1993)

- Less than one-fifth of all marriages in America were proceeded by marriage preparation courses. (McManus, 1993)

- In a study by Huber and Spitze in 1989, 1,360 husbands and wives were asked, "Has the thought of getting a divorce ever crossed your mind?" They found that more wives than husbands thought about divorce. How much each one earned had no effect on a spouse's thoughts of divorce. Nor did the attitudes about the roles of men and women. But the more housework a wife saw her husband do, the less likely she was to think of divorce. As the researchers noted, "For each of the five daily household tasks which the husband performs at least half the time, the wife is about 3% less likely to have thought of divorce." The five tasks defined as taking the most time in housework were meal preparation, food shopping, childcare, daily housework, and meal cleanup." (Bellah, 1991)

- There is evidence that couples with boys are less likely to divorce than couples with girls. The authors of this study demonstrated this phenomenon and argue that this is the result of the very great likelihood that mothers will get custody of minor children and the greater closeness of fathers to their sons than to their daughters. Hence, fathers with sons are more willing to keep their marriage together at given levels of marital discord than fathers with daughters. (Goldscheider and White, 1991)

- Recent studies estimate that about two out of three first marriages will end in divorce or separation. (Goldscheider and White, 1991)

- Couples who delay the arrival of the first child at least a period after marriage give themselves time to establish their relationship and their respective roles in the marriage. This reasoning suggests that couples who wait several years before becoming parents stand the best chance of a satisfying and lasting relationship over the long run. (Goldscheider and White, 1991)

- If current trends continue, less that half of all children born today will live continuously with their mother and father throughout childhood. (Goldscheider and White, 1991)

- Half of the single mothers in the U.S. live below the poverty level. (Whitehead, 1993)

- Divorce almost always brings a decline in the standard of living for the mother and children. (Whitehead, 1993)

- One study shows that about 38% of divorced mothers and their children move during the first year after divorce. (Whitehead, 1993)

- Growing up in an intact two-parent family is an important source of advantage for American children. Not only does the intact family protect the child from poverty and economic insecurity; it also provides greater non-economic investments of parental time, attention, and emotional support over the entire life course. (Whitehead, 1993)

Effects of Divorce on Children

- In 1989, psychologists Judith Wallerstein and Sandra Blakeslee claimed that almost half of the children of divorced parents experience long-term pain, worry, and insecurity that adversely affect their love and work relationships. (Coontz, 1992)

- Researchers who managed to disentangle the effects of divorce itself from the effects of a change in physical location, for example, found that dislocation was much more likely to interfere with school completion than parental separation. (Coontz, 1992)

- Adults in single-parent families tend to spend less time supervising homework or interacting with teachers. Single parents are more likely to get upset and angry when their children receive bad grades. (Coontz, 1992)

- No one suffers more from parental selfishness that children do. A million kids a year have their lives shattered by the divorce of their parents. Half of them will not see the parent who leaves in the first year after divorce. (McManus, 1993)

- By age eighteen, six children out of ten will live in a single-parent family, and half of those absent parents are not required even to provide child support. (McManus, 1993)

- Karl Zinmeister wrote in 1990, "There is a mountain of scientific evidence showing that when families disintegrate, children often end up with intellectual, physical, and emotional scars that persist for life." (McManus, 1993)

- 30% of children who live with never-married mothers have repeated a grade, compared to only 12% of those living with both biological parents. (McManus, 1993)

- Children from single-parent homes are twice as likely to have behavior disorders as children from two-parent homes. (McManus, 1993)

- Crime rates among juveniles are more "associated with family structure than either poverty or race." Neighborhoods with high percentages of single-parent household have high rates of violent crime and burglary. (McManus, 1993)

- Much of the escalating murder rate comes from out-of-wedlock kids being brought up in the streets rather than in homes. (McManus, 1993)

- The National Commission on Children concluded that divorce devastates children, "Depression, trouble getting along with parents and peers, misbehavior stemming from anger and

124

© 1998, YouthLight, Inc.

declining school performance are common and continue to worsen as they get older." (McManus, 1993)

- From, "Dan Quayle Was Right" by Barbara Dafoe Whitehead (The Atlantic, April, 1993)
  - Children in single-parent families are six times more likely to be poor.
  - A 1988 survey by the National Center for Health Statistics found that children in single-parent families are two to three times as likely as children in two-parent families to have emotional and behavioral problems. They are also more likely to drop out of high school, to get pregnant as teenagers, to abuse drugs, and to be in trouble with the law.
  - Compared with children in intact families, children from disrupted families are at a much higher risk for physical and sexual abuse.
  - Contrary to popular belief, many children do not "bounce back" after divorce. Difficulties that are associated with family breakup often persist into adulthood. Research shows that many children from disrupted families have a harder time achieving intimacy in a relationship, forming a stable marriage, or even holding a steady job.
  - Five years after divorce, more than a third of the children in the study experienced moderate or severe depression.
  - Girls in single-parent homes are also at much greater risk of precocious sexuality, teenage marriage, teenage pregnancy, non-marital birth, and divorce than are girls in two-parent families.
  - According to a Canadian study, preschool children in stepfamilies are 40 times as likely as children in intact families to suffer physical or sexual abuse.
  - Nationally, more that 70% of all juveniles in state reform institutions come from fatherless homes.
  - According to a study by the National Association of Elementary School Principals, 33% of two-parent elementary school students are ranked as high achievers, as compared with 17% of single-parent students.
  - The children in single-parent families are also more likely to be truant or late or to have disciplinary action taken against them.
  - Children in stepfamilies report lower educational aspirations on the part of their parents and lower levels of parental involvement with schoolwork.
  - A 1991 survey by the National Commission on Children showed that the parents in stepfamilies were less likely to be involved in a child's school life, including involvement in extracurricular activities, than either involved in such time-consuming activities as coaching a child's team, accompanying class trips, or helping with school projects.
  - "The great educational tragedy of our time is that many American children are failing in school, not because they are intellectually or physically impaired, but because they are emotionally incapacitated. In schools across the nation principals report a dramatic rise in the aggressive, acting-out behavior characteristics of children, especially boys who live in single-parent families."

- Michael Thompson, a member of Independent School Psychological Consultants and a psychologist who practices in Cambridge, Mass. points out, "We've had a thirty-year epidemic of divorce and a generation of shell-shocked children. We have only begun to understand the long-term effects of having so many busted-up families." (The Atlantic, June, 1991)

- Suicide has tripled among adolescents, from 3.6 deaths per 100,000 in 1960 to 10.2 deaths by 1986 - in the same time that divorces also tripled. A study of state and county data by the National Commission on Children over a 47 year period found that the regions with the highest divorce rates also had the highest suicide rates; in contrast, suicide rates were lowest in those states with the highest rates of church membership. (McManus, 1993)

- Even infants and toddlers can react negatively to divorce with sleep, toilet training and feeding problems. Preschoolers may start hitting or biting their playmates or throwing temper tantrums. Younger school-age kids may react with sadness, school phobia, bed-wetting, or hyperactivity. Meanwhile, older children and teens may feel depressed, lonely, devalued, rejected, hurt, anxious, or ashamed. (Foley and Nechas, 1993)

- Nearly 30 years ago, Daniel Patrick Moynihan observed: "From the wild Irish slums of the 19th century eastern seaboard to the riot-torn suburbs of Los Angeles, there is one unmistakable lesson in American history; a community that allows a large number of young men and women to grow up in broken families, dominated by women, never acquiring male authority . . . that community asks for and gets chaos." (The Atlantic, June 1990)

What Are Educators Saying?

- Samuel Sava, past head of the National Association of Elementary School Principals, blames the decline of American education on a "parenting deficit." he notes, "It's not better teachers, texts, or curricula that our children need most. . . we will never see lasting school reform until we see parent reform." (Coontz, 1992)

- "Why launch new school reforms when the real key to educational performance is whether a child comes from a two-parent family? Why experiment with a new anti-poverty program when the most important indicator of poverty is whether there are two parents at home?" (Coontz, 1992)

- In a recent article in Education Week, Harold Howe 2nd, former head of the U.S. Office of Education noted:
  - "How anyone could draft the goals of education in this country without an emphasis on families and communities is hard to understand." (Howe was referring to George Bush's educational goals discussed in 1990.)
  - "The first goal of education should be changed to carry the full message initiatives to support and educate families needing help with this responsibility."
  - "Americans must consciously see the family as educational institution and understand that the schools alone cannot provide all the stimulation and guidance young people need to mature successfully."
  - "A Nation At Risk in 1983 sought longer school hours, more tests, and more required subjects but had nothing to say about families until its final few pages, where it delivered a short lecture urging families to take a major interest in the learning of their kids. There was no recognition at all of the very changes in American families in recent years. In effect, that bellwether report assumed that families from Scarsdale and families from Harlem were equally capable of doing more for their youngsters." (Education Week, 2-3-93)

- In 1991, the Carnegie Foundation for the Advancement of Teaching surveyed more than 7,000 kindergarten teachers how well prepared their students were for formal education, focusing especially on physical well-being, social confidence, emotional maturity, language richness, general knowledge, and moral awareness - what we define as the key dimensions of school readiness. The results were deeply troubling. According to teachers, 35% of the nation's children were not ready for school. Even more disturbing, when asked how the readiness of last year's students compared to those enrolled five years ago, 42% of the teachers said that students were more deficient, teachers overwhelming cited, "lack of proficiency in language." In response to the question, "What would most improve the school readiness of children?", the majority said, "Parent education." (Boyer, 1991)

- "We begin, where we must, with parents. When all is said and done, mothers and fathers are the first and most essential teachers. It's in the home that children must be clothed, fed, and loved. This is the place where life's most basic lessons will be learned. No outside program - no surrogate or substitute arrangement - however well planned or well intended, can replace a supportive family that gives the child emotional security and a rich environment for learning." (Boyer, 1991)

- In 1993, the Metropolitan Life Insurance Company surveyed 1,000 teachers. Highlights from the survey include:
  - 69% of teachers believe that one of the federal government's highest priorities should be programs helping disadvantaged parents work with their children to encourage learning.
  - 86% of teachers feel that parents should be penalized through fines or some other mechanism for allowing their children to be chronically truant.
  - 42% of teachers feel parents should be penalized for refusing to attend parent-teacher conferences. (Metlife Survey, 1993)

- In Washington state, the Department of Social and Health Services found that the broadest, most consistent predictors of school failure, substance abuse, delinquency, and adolescent pregnancy were poverty and having parents, whether married or not, who had not graduated from high school. (Coontz, 1992)

- "Teachers find many children emotionally distracted, so upset and preoccupied by the explosive drama of their own family lives that they are unable to concentrate on such mundane matters as multiplication tables." (Whitehead, 1993)

- In response, many schools have turned to therapeutic remediation. A growing proportion of many school budgets is devoted to counseling and other psychological services. (Whitehead, 1993)

Education Over the Years

1745   The Massachusetts Assembly ordered that any child older than six who did not know the alphabet was to be removed to another family.

1848   Following is a partial list of punishments (lashes) used in a North Carolina school:

Rules of the School	Number of Lashes
....Boys and girls playing together	4
....Fighting	5
....Playing cards at school	10
....Climbing for every foot over 3 feet up a tree	1
....For drinking spirituous liquors at school	8
....Making swings and swinging on them	7
....For wearing long fingernails	2
....For not making a bow when you meet a person	4
....For hollowing and hooping going home	3
....For every word you miss in your Heart Lesson	1

1872   Rules for teachers in St. Augustine, Florida:

* Men teachers may take one evening a week for courting purposes, or two evenings a week if they go to church regularly.
* Women teachers who marry or engage in unseemly conduct will be dismissed.
* Any teacher who smokes, uses liquor in any form, frequents pool or public halls, or gets shaved in a barber shop will give good reason to suspect his worth, intention, integrity, and honesty.

1888   Because children supplied essential farm labor, the school year lasted barely 12 weeks, from thanksgiving through early spring. Men teachers earned an average of $42.43 a month, women made $38.14.

1893   A survey of Brooklyn schools listed 18 classes with 90-100 students. One class had 158.

1959   Following is a "Question & Answer" by A.S. Neill in his book, *Summerhill*.

Question: "Does correct home rearing counteract the wrong teaching of a school?

Answer: "In the main, yes. The voice of the home is more powerful than the voice of the school. If the home is free from fear and punishment, the child will not some to believe that the school is right. Parents should tell their children what they think of a wrong school. Too often parents have an absurd sense of loyalty to even the most stupid of school teachers."

1972 In their book, *Discipline and the Disruptive Child: A Practical Guide for Elementary Teachers*, authors Karlin and Berger gave teachers this plan to get two students to stop fighting . . . "Use your voice as a weapon. Shriek at the children. Shriek as loudly as you possibly can. Shriek in their ears, if possible. . . .If your shrieking has not helped, try the following procedure: Being very careful of your own safety, if you are able to, try to pull the hair of both combatants. . . ."

References

Bellah, Robert, <u>The Good Society</u>, 1991, Alfred Knopf, New York.

Boyer, Ernest, <u>Ready To Learn</u>, 1991, Carnegie Foundation, Princeton, NJ.

Bruskin-Goldring Research, EDUCATION WEEK, May 19, 1993.

Caplan, Arthur, Knight Rider, June 24, 1993.

Carnegie Corporation, "A Matter of Time: Risk and Opportunity in the Non-School Hours", 1992, Carnegie Corporation, New York.

Carr, Tom, <u>Keeping Love Alive in the Family</u>, 1992, Professional Press, Chapel Hill, NC.

Carr, Tom, "Student perceptions of non-school hours", 1993, Hillsborough, NC.

Carr, Tom, "What Are the Fears, Worries, Concerns of North Carolina eighth graders?", 1992, Carr Counseling & Consultation, Hillsborough, NC.

Children's Defense Fund, 1991, Annual Report, Washington, D.C.

Coontz, Stephanie, <u>The Way We Never Were</u>, 1992 Basic Books, New York.

Csikszentmihalyi, M. and Larson, R. 1984, <u>Being Adolescent: Conflict and Growth in the Teenage Years</u>, Basic Books, New York.

Csikszentmihalyi, M. and Rochberg-Halton, <u>Meaning of Things</u>, 1981, Cambridge University Press, Cambridge, England.

Fishman, Katherine, "Therapy For Children", THE ATLANTIC, June 1991.

Foley, Denise and Nechas, Eileen, <u>Women's Encyclopedia of Health and Emotional Healing</u>, 1993, Rodale Press, Emmaus, PA.

Glass, J. Conrad, "Death, loss, grief, among middle school children: Implications for the school counselor," Elementary School Guidance & Counseling, volume 26, Dec., 1991.

Goldscheider, Frances, and Waite, Linda, <u>New Families, No Families</u>, 1991, University of California Press, Los Angeles.

Hopper, G. and Christensen, M. "Identifying and Assisting Depressed Adolescents and Pre-Adolescents," American School Counselor Conference, 1991, Des Moines, Iowa,

Howe, Harold, "We Need Four More National Educational Goals," EDUCATION WEEK, February 3, 1993.

Liebert and Joyce Sprafkin, The Early Window, 1988, Pergamon Press, New York.

Metropolitan Life Survey, "The American Teacher,"1993, Louis Harris, New York.

McManus, Michael, The Marriage Savers, 1993, Zondervan Publishing, Grand Rapids, MI.

Nassar, C., Hodges, P., Ollendick, T., "Self-concept, eating disorders, and dietary patterns in young adolescent girls," School Counselor, Vol. 39, May 1992.

Newman, L. and Buka, S., "Every Child a Learner: Reducing Risks of Learning Impairment During Pregnancy and Infancy," 1990, Education Commission of the States, Denver.

Parker, Harvey, The ADD Hyperactivity Handbook for Schools, 1992, Impact Publications, Plantation, FL.

Pelton, L., "Child Abuse and Neglect: The Myth of Classlessness," American Journal of Orthopsychiatry, Vol. 48, 1978.

Radecki, D., "Cartoon Report", April 1991, National Coalition of Television Violence, Champaign, IL.

Simon, Paul, "Reducing Violence on Television," EDUCATION WEEK, October 4, , 1989.

Stinnet, N. and DeFrain, J., Secrets of Strong Families, 1986, Little and Brown, Boston.

Taras, H. et al, "Children's television viewing habits and the family environment," Journal of Diseases of Children, Vol. 144, March 1990.

Timmer, S., 1985, "How Children Use Time," University of Michigan, Ann Arbor.

USA TODAY, April 20, 1993

USA TODAY, May 3, 1990.

USA TODAY, June 8, 1993

USA TODAY, June 16, 1993

Whitehead, Barbara, "Dan Quayle Was Right.", THE ATLANTIC, April 1993.

Will, George, Washington Post, June 15, 1993.

Wilson, J. and Blocher, L. "The counselor's role in assisting children of alcoholics." Elementary School Guidance and Counseling, Vol. 25, Dec. 1990.

Woodside, M. "Children of Alcoholics: A Report to the Governor", 1992, Children of Alcoholics Foundations.

Zinsmeister, Karl, "Growing Up Scared, THE ATLANTIC, June 1990.

Books

Affective Enterprises (1987). Friendship. Callahan, FL.

Borba, M. and Borba, C. (1978). Self-Esteem: A Classroom Affair. Harper and Row.

Borba, M. (1989). Esteem Builders, Jalmar Press, California, 1989.

Brun, J., (1992). They can, but they don't: Helping students overcome work inhibition. New York: Viking.

Frey, Di. and C. Jesse Carlock, Enhancing Self-Esteem. Accelerated Development Inc., 1989 (1-800-222-1166).

From the editors of Group Publishing, Group Growers. Thom Schultz Publications, Inc. 1988.

Graves, F. (1989). Staff Development Workshop. Richland School District One, Columbia, SC

Hallinan, P.K. I'm Glad to be Me. Children's Press, Chicago, 1977.

Kreidler, W.J. (1984). Creative Conflict Resolution. Glenview, IL: Scott, Foresman, and Company.

Landy, L. (1988). Child Support (through small group counseling). Mount Dora, FL: Kidsrights.

Lesesne, T. (1986). I'm Special. Charlotte, NC: The Drug Education Center.

Lions-Quest, (1989). Training Curriculum: Skills for Growing. Rock Hill, SC: Quest International.

Muntean, Michaela. The Little Engine That Could. Platt and Munk Publishers, 1988.

Myrick, R.D. (1987). <u>Developmental Guidance and Counseling: A Practical Approach.</u> Minneapolis, MN: Educational Media Corporation.

Palmer, P. (1977). <u>The Mouse, Monster, and Me.</u> San Luis Obispo, CA: Impact Publishers

Phillips, Deborah, <u>How to Give your Child a Great Self-Esteem.</u> Random House, 1989.

<u>Pumsy, in Pursuit of Excellence</u> and <u>Pumsy, Bright Beginnings.</u> Timberline Press, (P.O. Box 70187, Eugene, Oregon, 97401).

Smith, S. and Walter, G. <u>Four Steps to Making Friends Training Manual.</u> Rock Hill, SC: Winthrop College.

Weinstein, M. and Goodman, J. (1980). <u>Playfair.</u> San Luis Obispo, CA: Impact Publishers.

Journals

Adams, W. (1989). The fruit basket. <u>PIC (Practical Ideas for Counselors)</u>, <u>2</u>, 6-7.

Cooper, J. and Martenz, J. (1989). Understanding differences, <u>PIC (Practical Ideas for Counselors)</u>, <u>2</u>, 3-4.

Sacharow-Nayowith, R. (1989). Prejudice, <u>PIC (Practical Ideas for Counselors)</u>, <u>2</u>, 3-4.

Other Suggested Resources

(Note: this list is not comprehensive or exhaustive. It represents materials on display, favorite materials used by the authors, and a few selected others.)

<u>Raising Self-Reliant Children In a Self Indulgent World</u>
    By H. Stephen Glenn and Jane Nelson
    Prima Publishing & Communications
    P.O. Box 1260 SR
    Rockling, CA 95677 (916) 624-5718

<u>Five Cries of Parents: New Help for Families on the Issues that Trouble Them Most</u>
    By Merton P. Strommen & A. Irene Strommen
    Harper & Row Publishers, Inc.
    10 East 53rd Street
    New York, NY 10022

How Children Fail
    By John Holt
    Dell Publishing Co., Inc.
    750 Third Avenue, New York, NY 10017

Control Theory in the Classroom
    By William Glasser, M.D.
    Harper & Row, Publishers, Inc.
    10 East 53rd St., New York, NY 10022

Control Theory: A New Explanation of How We Control Our Lives
    By William Glasser, M.D.
    Harper & Row, Publishers, Inc.
    10 East 53rd St., New York, NY 10022

Games People Play
    By Eric Berne, M.D.
    Grove Press, Inc.
    New York, NY

Depression in Young People
    Edited by M. Rutler, C.E. Izard, & P.B. Read
    The Guilford Press
    200 Park Avenue South
    New York, NY 10003

The Acting-Out Child: Coping with Classroom Disruption
    By Hill M. Walker
    Allyn and Bacon, Inc.
    470 Atlantic Avenue
    Boston, MA 02210

Coping with Difficult People
    By Robert M. Bramson
    Doubleday
    666 Fifth Avenue
    New York, NY 10103

Winning Children Over: A Manual for Teachers, Counselors, Principals and Parents
    By Francis X. Walton & Robert L. Powers
    Adlerian Childcare Books
    Box 210206
    Columbia, SC 29221

Between Parent & Teenager
    By Haim Ginott
    Macmillan Publishing Company
    866 Third Avenue
    New York, NY 10022

Between Teacher and Child
    By Haim Ginott
    Avon Books
    105 Madison Avenue
    New York, NY 10016

People Making
    By Virginia Satir
    Science and Behavior Books, Inc.
    Palo Alto, CA

All Grown Up and No Place to Go The Hurried Child Children and Adolescents
    By David Elkind
    Alfred A. Knopf, Inc.
    New York, NY

How to Help Children with Common Problems
    Schaefer, C.E., Millman, H.L.
    The Mosby Press
    The C.V. Mosby Company
    11830 Westline Industrial Drive
    St. Louis, MO 63141

Positive Discipline
    By Jane Nelsen
    Ballentine Books
    Random House, Inc.
    New York, NY

Discipline without Tears
    By Rudolf Dreikurs and Cassel, Pearl
    E.P. Dutton, Inc.
    2 Park Avenue
    New York, NY 10016

Teaching/Discipline
    By Madsen, C.H., Madson, C.K.
    Allyn & Bacon, Inc.
    470 Atlantic Avenue
    Boston, MA

Discipline and the Disruptive Child
    By Kaslin, M., and Berger, R.
    Parker Publishing Company, Inc.
    West Nyack, NY

Children: The Challenge
    By Dreikurs, R.
    E.P. Dulton
    2 Park Avenue
    New York, NY 10016

Six Point Plan for Raising Happy, Healthy Children
    By Rosemond, John
    Anderson and McNeel, A Universal Press Syndicate Company
    4900 Main Street
    Kansas City, MO 64122

Dare to Discipline The Strong-Willed Child
    By Dobson, James
    Tyndale House Publishers, Inc.
    Wheaton, Illinois 60187

Winning the Homework War
    By Levine, F.M. and Anesko, K.M.
    Prentiss-Hall Press
    A Division of Session and Sebustu, Inc.
    Gulf and Western Building
    One Gulf and Western Place
    New York, NY 10023

How to Talk So Kids Will Listen and Listen So Kids Will Talk
    By Faber, Adele and Elaine Mozlisk
    Avon Books, A Division of The Hearst Corporation
    105 Madison Avenue
    New York, NY 10016

Feeling Good About Me
    By Kenneth Morrison and Monica Thompson
    Educational Media Corporation
    P.O. Box 21311
    Minneapolis, Minnesota 55421

Your Child's Self-Esteem
    By Dorothy Cookville Briggs
    A Dolphin Book
    Bantam Doubleday Dell Publishing Co., Inc.
    666 Fifth Avenue. New York, NY 10103

The Other Side of the Report Card
    By Larry Chase
    Paperbacks for Educators
    1240 Ridge Road
    Ballwin, Missouri 63021 (800) 227-2591 MO (314) 227-2590

100 Ways to Enhance Self-Concept in the Classroom
    By Jack Canfield and Harold Wells
    Prentiss Hall, Inc.
    Englewood Cliffs, NJ

Life 101
    By John Roger, Peter McWilliams
    Prelude Press
    8165 Mannix Drive
    Los Angeles, CA 90046

Helping Children Choose
    By George M. Schuncke and Susan Lowell Krogh
    Scott, Foresman, and Company
    Glenview, Illinois 60025

Energizers and Icebreakers
    By Elizabeth S. Foster
    Educational Media Corporation
    P.O. Box 21311
    Minneapolis, Minnesota 55421

Substance Abuse Prevention Activities for Elementary Children
    By Timothy A. Gerne, Jr. , Patrick J. Gerne
    Prentice-Hall Inc.
    Englewood Cliffs, NJ

How to Talk to Children about Really Important Things
    By Charles E. Shaefer
    Paperbacks for Educators
    Washington, Missouri 63090 (800) 227-2591   (314) 239-1999

Games Children Should Play
    By Mary K. Cihak, Barbara J. Heron
    Paperbacks for Educators
    1240 Ridge Rd.
    Ballwin, Baldwin, MO 63021

Belonging
    By Jayne Devencenzi and Susan Pendergast
    2960 Hawk Hill Lane
    San Luis Obispo CA 95401

Helping Children Cope with Separation and Loss
    By Claudia L. Jewett
    The Harvard Common Press, Inc.
    535 Albany Street
    Boston, MA 02118

© 1998, YouthLight, Inc.

A Survival Guide for the Elementary/Middle School Counselor
By John J. Schmidt
The Center for Applied Research in Education, Inc.
Business Information Publishing Div.
West Nyack, NY 10995

Counseling Young Students at Risk
By Jeanne C. Bleur and Penny A. Schrieber
ERU Counseling and Personnel Services Clearinghouse
2108 School of Education
The University of Michigan
Ann Arbor, Michigan 48109-1259

The Compassionate School
By Gertrude Morrow
Prentiss-Hall, Inc.
Englewood Cliffs, NJ

Free Catalogs of Materials
Available on Related Topics

Sunburst Communications
Fax: 914-747-4109 Toll Free: 800-431-1934
101Castlenton St.
P.O. Box 100
Pleasantville, NY 10570-0040

Childswork/Childsplay
100 Plaza Dr.
Secausus, NJ 07094 1-800-962-1141

Mar-co Products, Inc.
1443 Old York Road
Warminster, PA 18974 1-800-448-2197

Negotiation Institute Inc.
341 Madison Avenue, 20th Floor
New York, NY 10017-3705 (212) 986-5555 FAX: (212) 599-3077

Kidsrights
10100 Park Cedar Drive
Charlotte, NC 28210
1-800-892-KIDS (704) 541-0100 FAX: 704-541-0113

NIMCO. INC.
102 Hwy. 81 N.
P.O. Box 9
Calhoun, KY 42327-009 1-800-962-6662 FAX: 502-273-5844

American Guidance Service
4201 Woodland Road
P.O. Box 99
Circle Pines, MN 55014-1796 1-800-328-2560 FAX: 612-786-9077

National School Products
10 East Broadway
Maryville, TN 37081-37804 (615) 984-3960 1-800-627-9393 FAX: 1-800-289-3960

Ready Reference Press
P.O. Box 5249
Santa Monica, CA 90409 1-800-424-5627 FAX: 1-310-475-4895

Paperbacks for Educators
426 West Front Street
Washington, MO 63090 1-800-227-2591 (314) 239-1999 FAX: 314-239-4515

J. Weston Walch, Publisher
321 Valley Street
P.O. Box 658
Portland, Maine 04104-0658 1-800-341-6094 FAX: 1-207-772-3105

CFKR Career Marerials, Inc.
11860 Kemper Road, Unit 7
Auburn, CA 95603 1-800-525-5626 FAX: 916-889-0433

Social Studies School Service
10200 Jefferson Blvd. Room M011
P.O. Box 802
Culver City, CA 90232-0802 1-800-421-4246 FAX: 310-839-2249

Education Media Corporation
4256 Central Ave.
Minneapolis, MN 55421-0311 1-800-966-3382

About the Authors

Robert P. Bowman, Ph.D., is a former teacher, counselor, and professional entertainer who makes each of his presentations extremely practical and fun. Dr. Bowman is currently an Associate Professor in the Department of Educational Psychology at the University of South Carolina. He has written 15 nationally recognized books and programs that relate to motivating students from grades K-12.

Tom Carr, M.S., is a much sought-after consultant who has presented more than a hundred workshops to educators and other professional groups. He is a unique presenter whose workshops are "high energy," entertaining, and impelling. Participants leave his workshops feeling energized and filled with useful ideas they can take back to their schools and use immediately. Tom is the author of the book, *Keeping Love Alive in the Family* which is a practical guide to building a more harmonious family life. In addition, Tom has written, *150 Ways to Keep Your Lover, A Parents Blueprint,* and *Monday Morning Messages* along with several professional articles for educators and parents.

Kathy Cooper, M.S.W., is known as an outstanding presenter with an extensive collection of creative and useful strategies for working with many different types of difficult youth. People leave her workshops feeling "energized" and "full of many fresh ideas and strategies." Kathy has worked with difficult youth as a social worker and school counselor where she has been developing strategies that lead to real-and-lasting positive changes in the attitudes, beliefs, and behaviors of difficult students. She is the co-author of *Power Play* and *Quality Times for Quality Kids.*

Ron Miles, Ph.D., is an inspirational speaker and workshop leader who has presented motivational workshops for educators around the United States. Participants leave his workshops with an extensive collection of practical strategies and activities they can use with students. He is especially known for his work with alternative approaches for "cutting through" to difficult youth. Ron is the Director of Guidance for an inner-city school district and Adjunct Professor in the Department of Educational Psychology at the University of South Carolina. He has won several state and national awards for his dedication to helping youth. In 1998 he was named National Guidance Administrator of the Year by the American School Counselor Association.